KT-224-182

# Cakes

BLOOMSBURY KITCHEN LIBRARY

# Cakes

Bloomsbury Books
London

This edition published 1994 by Bloomsbury Books,
an imprint of The Godfrey Cave Group,
42 Bloomsbury Street, London, WC1B 3QJ.

All rights reserved. No part of this publication may be reproduced,
stored in a retrieval system, or transmitted, in any form or by any
means, electronic, mechanical, photocopying, recording or
otherwise without the prior permission of the copyright holder.

© 1994 Time-Life Books B.V.

ISBN 1 85471 507 0

Printed and bound in Great Britain.

# Contents

# Pastry Cream Variations

**Makes
60 cl (1 pint)**

**Working
time: about
20 minutes**

**Total time:
about
4 hours**

| 60 g | cornflour | 2 oz | 1 tsp | pure vanilla extract | 1 tsp |
| 60 g | caster sugar | 2 oz | 1 | egg white (optional) | 1 |
| 60 cl | skimmed milk | 1 pint | 60 g | thick Greek yogurt | 2 oz |

Blend the cornflour in a bowl with the sugar and 2 tablespoons of the milk. Pour the remaining milk into a saucepan and bring it to the boil. Pour the boiling milk on to the blended cornflour, stirring continuously. Pour the custard back into the saucepan and cook over a low heat, stirring, for 6 to 8 minutes until every trace of raw cornflour has gone. Beat in the vanilla extract. Strain the custard through a nylon sieve into a clean bowl and cover the surface closely with plastic film to prevent a skin from forming. Allow the pastry cream to cool, then refrigerate it for 2 to 3 hours, or overnight, until it is completely cold.

Whisk the cold custard until it is very smooth. Whisk the egg white until it forms soft peaks. Fold the yogurt into the custard, then gradually fold in the egg white. Cover the bowl and return the pastry cream to the refrigerator to chill thoroughly.

*Liqueur-flavoured pastry cream.* Stir 4 tablespoons of brandy, rum or a liqueur such as kirsch into the custard at the same time as the vanilla extract.

*Orange-flavoured pastry cream.* Add the grated rind of 2 oranges to the cold milk in the saucepan. In place of the vanilla extract, add 2 tablespoons of Grand Marnier.

*Coffee-flavoured pastry cream.* Stir 2 tablespoons of very strong black coffee into the custard with the vanilla extract.

*Chocolate-flavoured pastry cream.* Add 2 tablespoons of cocoa powder to the initial blend of cornflour, sugar and milk.

*Almond pastry cream.* Beat 60 g (2 oz) of ground almonds and 3 drops of almond extract into the custard at the same time as the Greek yogurt.

# Frosted Orange Cake

Serves 14

Working time: about 25 minutes

Total time: about 3 hours and 30 minutes

Calories 214

Protein 3g

Cholesterol 30mg

Total fat 7g

Saturated fat 2g

Sodium 100mg

| | | |
|---|---|---|
| 300 g | plain flour | 10 oz |
| 2¼ tsp | baking powder | 2¼ tsp |
| 125 g | polyunsaturated margarine | 4 oz |
| 90 g | light brown sugar | 3 oz |
| 2 | oranges, grated rind only | 2 |
| 2 | eggs | 2 |

| | | |
|---|---|---|
| 3 tbsp | fresh orange juice | 3 tbsp |
| | **Orange Glacé Icing** | |
| 125 g | icing sugar | 4 oz |
| 3 tsp | fresh orange juice | 3 tsp |
| ½ | orange, grated rind only | ½ |

Preheat the oven to 170°C (325°F or Mark 3). Line an 18 cm (7 inch) round cake tin with non-stick parchment paper.

Sift the flour and baking powder together into a bowl and rub in the margarine until the mixture resembles fine breadcrumbs. Stir in the sugar and orange rind. In another bowl, beat the eggs and fresh orange juice together and then mix them into the dry ingredients with a wooden spoon. Turn the batter into the prepared tin and level the top. Bake the cake for about 1 hour,

until well risen and firm to the touch; a skewer inserted in the centre of the cake should come out clean. Turn the cake on to a wire rack, leave it until cool and then peel off the paper.

To make the icing, sift the icing sugar into a bowl and beat in just enough of the orange juice to give a thick coating consistency. Spread the icing over the top of the cake, allowing it to run down the sides in places. Sprinkle the icing with the grated orange rind and leave the cake until the icing has set.

# Coffee Sandwich

Serves 12

Working time: about 30 minutes

Total time: about 2 hours and 15 minutes

Calories 190
Protein 3g
Cholesterol 45mg
Total fat 9g
Saturated fat 3g
Sodium 160mg

| | | |
|---|---|---|
| 125 g | polyunsaturated margarine | 4 oz |
| 125 g | light brown sugar | 4 oz |
| 2 | eggs | 2 |
| 60 g | wholemeal flour | 2 oz |
| 125 g | plain flour | 4 oz |
| 1¾ tsp | baking powder | 1¾ tsp |

| | | |
|---|---|---|
| 1 tbsp | black treacle | 1 tbsp |
| 1 tbsp | very strong black coffee | 1 tbsp |
| 15 cl | coffee-flavoured pastry cream (see page 7) | ¼ pint |
| 2 tbsp | icing sugar | 2 tbsp |

Preheat the oven to 190°C (375°F or Mark 5). Grease two 20 cm (8 inch) round sandwich tins and line their bases with non-stick parchment paper.

Cream the margarine and brown sugar together in a bowl until pale and fluffy. With a wooden spoon, beat in the eggs one at a time, following each with 1 tablespoon of the wholemeal flour. Sift the plain flour with the baking powder and mix it with the remaining wholemeal flour; then add the flours to the creamed mixture, alternating them with the black treacle and coffee. Divide the batter between the prepared tins and level the tops. Cook the sponges for 20 to 25 minutes,

until well risen and firm to the touch. Turn them out on to a wire rack, leave them until completely cooled and then peel off the paper.

To assemble the cake, stand one sponge layer on a serving plate and spread the coffee-flavoured pastry cream (see page 7) evenly over it. Cover it with the second sponge layer, then sift the icing sugar over the cake. Heat a skewer until it is red hot and use it to brand a lattice pattern on the cake. To soften the contrast between the brand marks and the rest of the surface, complete the decoration with a second, very light dusting of icing sugar.

# Chiffon Cake with Raspberry-Cream Filling

| | | |
|---|---|---|
| **Serves 16** | | **Calories**<br>210 |
| | | **Protein**<br>3g |
| **Working<br>time: about<br>35 minutes** | | **Cholesterol**<br>45mg |
| | | **Total fat**<br>9g |
| **Total time:<br>about<br>1 hour and<br>20 minutes** | | **Saturated fat**<br>2g |
| | | **Sodium**<br>110mg |

| | | | | | |
|---|---|---|---|---|---|
| **175 g** | plain flour | **6 oz** | | **Fruit and Cream Filling** | |
| **3 tsp** | baking powder | **3 tsp** | **75 g** | caster sugar | **2½ oz** |
| **125 g** | caster sugar, plus 1 tbsp | **4 oz** | **4** | fresh peaches, sliced | **4** |
| **3 tbsp** | safflower oil | **3 tbsp** | **2 tbsp** | brandy | **2 tbsp** |
| **3** | egg yolks | **3** | **¼ litre** | whipping cream | **8 fl oz** |
| **6** | egg whites | **6** | **125 g** | fresh raspberries | **4 oz** |

Preheat oven to 170°C (325°F or Mark 3). Grease two 20 cm (8 inch) sandwich tins. Line the bases with greased greaseproof paper.

Sift flour and baking powder and mix in 125 g (4 oz) of sugar. Make a well in the centre. In another bowl, whisk oil and egg yolks with 5 tbsps of water until blended. Pour into dry ingredients and beat to create a smooth batter.

Whisk egg whites until stiff but not dry. Fold one third of whites into batter using a large metal spoon. Carefully fold in the remaining whites.

Divide the mixture between two tins, tapping to level. Bake in centre of oven, until well risen, lightly browned and springy to touch – about 20 minutes. Turn sponges out onto a wire rack and remove the paper. Leave until completely cool.

Slowly heat 60 g (2 oz) of the sugar and 15 cl (¼ pint) of water together in a pan, stirring until sugar dissolves. Reduce by boiling gently for 4 – 5 minutes. Simmer the peach slices in the syrup for 1 – 2 minutes to soften slightly. Drain the slices on kitchen paper before peeling. Stir 1 tablespoon of brandy into the syrup. Whisk remaining sugar and brandy until cream holds soft peaks.

Set one sponge layer on a plate. Spread half the syrup over the sponge, then half the cream.

Spread the remaining syrup over the bottom of the second sponge, then invert it onto the first. Sift the caster sugar over the cake.

# Streusel Ring

**Serves 16**

**Working time: about 25 minutes**

**Total time: about 3 hours and 30 minutes**

Calories 230

Protein 3g

Cholesterol 35mg

Total fat 10g

Saturated fat 4g

Sodium 145mg

| | | |
|---|---|---|
| **300 g** | plain flour | **10 oz** |
| **2¼ tsp** | baking powder | **2½ tsp** |
| **125 g** | polyunsaturated margarine | **4 oz** |
| **60 g** | shredded coconut | **2 oz** |
| **90 g** | light brown sugar | **3 oz** |
| **2** | limes, grated rind only | **2** |
| **2** | eggs | **2** |
| **2 tbsp** | clear honey | **2 tbsp** |

| | | |
|---|---|---|
| **4 tbsp** | skimmed milk | **4 tbsp** |
| | **Coconut Streusel Topping** | |
| **60 g** | wholemeal flour | **2 oz** |
| **30 g** | polyunsaturated margarine | **1 oz** |
| **30 g** | demerara sugar | **1 oz** |
| **1 tbsp** | shredded coconut | **1 tbsp** |

Preheat the oven to 180°C (350°F or Mark 4). Thoroughly grease a tubular springform cake tin approximately 22 cm (9 inches) in diameter.

Sift the flour and baking powder into a bowl and rub in the margarine until the mixture resembles fine breadcrumbs. Mix in the coconut, sugar and lime rind. Put the eggs, honey and milk into a small bowl and whisk them together, then beat them into the dry ingredients with a wooden spoon. Turn the batter into the prepared tin and level the top.

To make the streusel topping, put the flour into a bowl and rub in the margarine. Mix in the sugar and shredded coconut. Sprinkle the blend evenly over the top of the batter. Cook the streusel ring for about 1 hour, until well risen and firm; a skewer inserted in the centre should come out clean. Leave the cake in the tin for 5 minutes to allow it to shrink from the sides, then release the spring and turn the cake out carefully on to a wire rack to cool.

# Pistachio Battenburg Cake

Serves 16

Working time: about 1 hour

Total time: about 14 hours

Calories 250

Protein 3g

Cholesterol 30mg

Total fat 12g

Saturated fat 2g

Sodium 180mg

| | | |
|---|---|---|
| 125 g | polyunsaturated margarine | 4 oz |
| 125 g | light brown sugar | 4 oz |
| 2 | eggs | 2 |
| 175 g | plain flour | 6 oz |
| 1½ tsp | baking powder | 1½ tsp |
| 2 tsp | strong black coffee | 2 tsp |
| 1 tsp | cocoa powder, sieved | 1 tsp |

| | | |
|---|---|---|
| 3 tbsp | apricot jam without added sugar | 3 tbsp |
| | **Pistachio Marzipan** | |
| 175 g | shelled pistachio nuts | 6 oz |
| 90 g | caster sugar | 3 oz |
| 90 g | icing sugar, sifted | 3 oz |
| 1 tsp | fresh lemon juice | 1 tsp |
| 1 | egg white, lightly beaten | 1 |

For marzipan, blanch nuts for 2 mins in simmering water. Drain, enfold in a towel and rub to loosen skins; peel. Dry on kitchen paper for several hours.

Preheat oven to 180°C (350°F or Mark 4). Line a rectangular tin 28 by 18 by 4 cm (11 by 7 by 1½ inches) with non-stick parchment paper, with a deep crosswise pleat dividing the tin into two halves.

Cream the margarine and brown sugar in a bowl until pale and fluffy. Beat in eggs one at a time, following each with 1 tablespoon of flour. Sift remaining flour and baking powder together and fold into the mixture.

Split mixture into two bowls. Into one, beat the coffee; into the other, beat cocoa powder and 2 teaspoons of water. Spoon coffee mixture into one side of the tin and chocolate into the other. Cook

sponges for 20 to 25 minutes, until firm to touch. Turn out on a wire rack, remove lining paper and leave to cool.

Grate the pistachios finely into a bowl. Add caster sugar and icing sugar. Mix in lemon juice and enough beaten egg white to give a firm, pliable consistency.

Trim the sponges to the same size and cut each in half lengthwise. Join sponges together with jam to make chequer-board cross-section.

Dust the marzipan liberally with icing sugar and roll it into a rectangle – about 30 cm by 22 cm (12 by 9 inches). Cover sponge with a thin layer of jam and wrap in marzipan. Trim the ends.

Decorate top in criss-cross pattern with a sharp knife. Allow to dry uncovered overnight.

# Chocolate Marble Cake

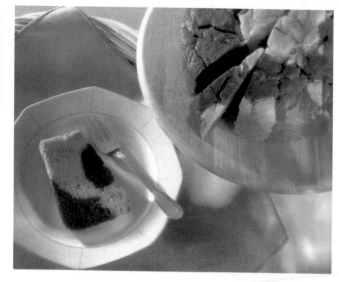

Serves 20

Working time: about 20 minutes

Total time: about 3 hours

Calories 215
Protein 3g
Cholesterol 60mg
Total fat 13g
Saturated fat 5g
Sodium 145mg

| | | | |
|---|---|---|---|
| **350 g** | plain flour | **12 oz** | |
| **3 tsp** | baking powder | **3 tsp** | |
| **175 g** | caster sugar | **6 oz** | |
| **150 g** | unsalted butter | **5 oz** | |

| | | | |
|---|---|---|---|
| **125 g** | polyunsaturated margarine | **4 oz** | |
| **4** | eggs | **4** | |
| **1½ tbsp** | cocoa powder | **1½ tbsp** | |

Preheat the oven to 170°C (325°F or Mark 3). Grease a 20 cm (8 inch) round cake tin. Line the tin with greaseproof paper and grease the paper.

Sift the flour and baking powder into a mixing bowl. Add the sugar, butter, margarine and eggs. Mix them together, then beat the batter with a wooden spoon for 2 to 3 minutes until it is smooth and glossy. Transfer half of the batter to another bowl.

Dissolve the cocoa in 3 tablespoons of boiling water and blend the paste until it is smooth. Add the cocoa mixture to one of the bowls of batter and stir to incorporate it. Then transfer alternate spoonfuls of plain and chocolate batter to the prepared cake tin. Tap the tin to level the batter and swirl a skewer through it to create a marbled effect.

Bake the cake in the centre of the oven, until risen, lightly browned and springy when touched in the centre – 50 to 55 minutes. Loosen the edges with a small palette knife, turn the cake out of the tin on to a wire rack and remove the lining paper. Leave the cake to cool completely.

*Editor's Note:* To vary the chocolate marble cake, add 1 teaspoon of grated orange rind to the plain batter. To make a coffee marble cake, replace the dissolved cocoa with 3 tablespoons of very strong black coffee.

# Apricot and Pine-Nut Roll

Serves 12

Working time: about 40 minutes

Total time: about 1 hour and 15 minutes

Calories 145

Protein 5g

Cholesterol 35mg

Total fat 5g

Saturated fat 0g

Sodium 50mg

| 175 g | dried apricots | 6 oz | 60 g | brown flour | 2 oz |
|---|---|---|---|---|---|
| 30 cl | fresh orange juice | ½ pint | ½ tsp | baking powder | ½ tsp |
| 2 tbsp | plain low-fat yogurt | 2 tbsp | 90 g | pine-nuts, finely ground | 3 oz |
| 2 | eggs | 2 | 2 | egg whites | 2 |
| 60 g | light brown sugar | 2 oz | 1 tbsp | caster sugar | 1 tbsp |

Preheat oven to 180°C (350°F or Mark 4). Grease a 32 by 22 cm (13 by 9 inch) Swiss roll tin. Line it with greaseproof paper and grease the paper.

Put apricots and orange juice in a saucepan. Bring to the boil and simmer apricots for about 10 minutes, until tender and have absorbed nearly all juice. Leave to cool for 10 minutes; purée with yogurt. Set aside.

Put the eggs and brown sugar in a bowl set over a pan of hot, but not boiling, water. Whisk until the mixture is thick and creamy. Remove the bowl from the pan and continue to whisk until the whisk, when lifted, leaves a trail on the surface. Sift flour and baking powder into another bowl, and mix in 60 g (2 oz) of the pine-nuts. In a third bowl, whisk the egg whites until stiff, but not dry. Fold flour mixture, together with one third of the whites, into whisked eggs and sugar.

Fold in remaining whites.

Pour mixture into prepared tin and tap tin against work surface to level. Bake the batter in centre of oven for 10 to 15 minutes, until well risen, lightly browned and springy when touched in centre. Meanwhile, place a piece of greaseproof paper on the work surface. Mix the remaining pine-nuts with the caster sugar and sprinkle them evenly on the paper.

As soon as cake comes out oven, invert it on to the nuts. Working quickly, detach the lining paper from the cake and trim away the crisp edges on all four sides. Spread the apricot purée to the edge of the long sides and to within 5 mm (¼ inch) of the short sides. Using the paper, roll the cake up, starting at one short side. Grip the roll for 30 seconds, until it holds its shape. Put the roll on a wire rack to cool.

# Angel Cake Casket with Mango Filling

Serves 8

Working time: about 30 minutes

Total time: about 5 hours

Calories 150
Protein 3g
Cholesterol 0mg
Total fat 1g
Saturated fat 0g
Sodium 40mg

| | | |
|---|---|---|
| **5** | egg whites | **5** |
| **⅛ tsp** | salt | **⅛ tsp** |
| **175 g** | caster sugar | **6 oz** |
| **½** | lemon, finely grated rind only | **½** |
| **1 tbsp** | fresh lemon juice | **1 tbsp** |
| **30 g** | plain flour | **1 oz** |

| | | |
|---|---|---|
| **30 g** | cornflour | **1 oz** |
| | icing sugar to decorate | |
| | **Mango Filling** | |
| **1** | mango | **1** |
| **90 g** | fromage frais | **3 oz** |
| **1½ tsp** | gelatine | **1½ tsp** |

Preheat oven to 180°C (350°F or Mark 4). Lightly grease a 22 by 12 cm (9 by 5 inch) loaf tin. Line base with greaseproof paper and grease paper.

Whisk egg whites with salt until whites stand in stiff peaks. Whisk in 125 g (4 oz) of the caster sugar, 1 tablespoon at a time, until mixture is thick and glossy, whisk in the lemon rind and juice. Mix the remaining caster sugar with the flours and whisk this in, 1 tablespoon at a time.

Transfer mixture to prepared tin and bake it for 35 to 40 minutes until the cake is risen and firm to the touch. Leave it to cool in the tin.

Meanwhile, make filling. Peel mango and cut all flesh away from stone. Purée fruit in a food processor or blender: there should be about 20 cl (7 fl oz). Mix the purée with the *fromage frais*. Sprinkle the gelatine on to 2 tablespoons of hot water in a small bowl and stand the bowl in a pan of simmering water for about 10 minutes. When the gelatine has absorbed the water, add a little of the fruit mixture to it. Stir the gelatine-fruit mixture into the bulk of the purée.

Cut down into the cake 2 cm (¾ inch) from the sides to within 2 cm (¾ inch) of the base. Scoop out the centre of the cake with a spoon, to leave a casket with walls and base about 2 cm (¾ inch) thick. Pour the mango purée into the casket. Cover the purée with some of the angel cake trimmings to give the cake its original depth. Cover the cake with plastic film and chill it for at least 2 hours to allow the purée to set.

Using a palette knife, loosen the edges of the cake and invert it on to a platter. Dust with the icing sugar.

# Saffron Bun

Serves 20

Working time: about 40 minutes

Total time: about 14 hours

Calories 160

Protein 3g

Cholesterol 10mg

Total fat 4g

Saturated fat 2g

Sodium 10mg

| | | | |
|---|---|---|---|
| ¼ tsp | saffron threads | ¼ tsp | |
| 500 g | strong plain flour | 1 lb | |
| ⅛ tsp | salt | ⅛ tsp | |
| 90 g | unsalted butter | 3 oz | |
| 30 g | light brown sugar | 1 oz | |
| 1 | lemon, grated rind only | 1 | |
| 175 g | currants | 6 oz | |
| 30 g | mixed candied peel, chopped | 1 oz | |
| 15 g | fresh yeast, or 7 g (¼ oz) dried yeast plus 1 tsp caster sugar | ½ oz | |
| 15 cl | skimmed milk, tepid | ¼ pint | |
| 1 tbsp | clear honey | 1 tbsp | |

Infuse the saffron threads in 15 cl (¼ pint) of boiling water overnight, then strain the liquid and set it aside. Grease a 20 cm (8 inch) round cake tin.

Sift the flour and salt into a bowl and rub in the butter until the mixture resembles fine breadcrumbs. Stir in the sugar, lemon rind, currants and mixed peel. Blend the fresh yeast or the dried yeast and sugar with the milk. If you use dried yeast, leave the mixture in a warm place for about 15 minutes until frothy.

Warm the saffron liquid in a small saucepan and mix it, together with the yeast blend, into the dry ingredients. Turn the dough out on to a floured surface and knead it for about 5 minutes.

Shape the dough to fit the prepared tin. Put the dough in the tin and cover it with oiled plastic film. Leave it in a warm place for 1 to 1½ hours until it has doubled in size and springs back when lightly pressed with a floured finger. Meanwhile, preheat the oven to 200°C (400°F or Mark 6).

Remove the plastic film and bake the bun for 30 minutes. Reduce the temperature to 180°C (350°F or Mark 4) and bake the bun for 25 to 30 minutes more, until it is well risen, browned and firm to the touch. Turn the bun out on to a wire rack. While the bun is still warm, brush its top all over with a wet pastry brush dipped in the clear honey. Leave the bun to cool.

# Caraway Seed Sponge

Serves 12

Working time: about 25 minutes

Total time: about 3 hours and 30 minutes

Calories 125

Protein 3g

Cholesterol 60mg

Total fat 3g

Saturated fat 0g

Sodium 70mg

| | | |
|---|---|---|
| 3 | eggs, separated | 3 |
| 150 g | light brown sugar | 5 oz |
| 125 g | plain flour | 4 oz |
| 1 tsp | baking powder | 1 tsp |
| 1½ tbsp | cornflour | 1½ tbsp |

| | | |
|---|---|---|
| 2 tsp | polyunsaturated margarine | 2 tsp |
| 1 tbsp | orange flower water | 1 tbsp |
| 1 tsp | caraway seeds | 1 tsp |
| | icing sugar to decorate | |

Preheat the oven to 200°C (400°F or Mark 6). Grease a 20 cm (8 inch) round cake tin or a petal cake tin approximately 18 cm (7 inches) in diameter. Line the tin with non-stick parchment paper.

Whisk the egg whites until they stand in firm peaks. Gradually whisk in the brown sugar, 1 tablespoon at a time, then quickly fold in the egg yolks. Sift the flour, baking powder and cornflour together two or three times into another bowl to aerate them very thoroughly. Heat the margarine in a small saucepan until it melts then remove the pan from the heat and add the orange flower water and 2 tablespoons of water. Using a metal spoon or a rubber spatula, fold the flour mixture quickly and evenly into the cake mixture, followed by the melted mixture and the caraway seeds. Pour the batter into the prepared tin and bake, until well risen, golden-brown and firm to the touch – 25 to 30 minutes in the round tin, or 30 to 40 minutes in the petal tin.

Turn the cake out on to a wire rack and leave it to cool, then remove the paper. Before serving the cake, sift icing sugar lightly over the top.

# Ginger Kugelhopf

Serves 12

Working
time: about
40 minutes

Total time:
about
4 hours

Calories
167

Protein
4g

Cholesterol
80mg

Total fat
7g

Saturated fat
3g

Sodium
115mg

| | | |
|---|---|---|
| **15 g** | fresh yeast, or 7 g (¼ oz) dried yeast | **½ oz** |
| **30 g** | caster sugar | **1 oz** |
| **250 g** | strong plain flour | **8 oz** |
| **½ tsp** | salt | **½ tsp** |
| **1 tsp** | ground cinnamon | **1 tsp** |
| **½ tsp** | ground ginger | **½ tsp** |

| | | |
|---|---|---|
| **60 g** | unsalted butter, melted | **2 oz** |
| **3** | eggs, beaten | **3** |
| **30 g** | stem ginger, finely chopped | **1 oz** |
| **30 g** | dried apricots, finely chopped | **1 oz** |
| **30 g** | plain chocolate | **1 oz** |
| **2 tsp** | pine-nuts | **2 tsp** |

Mix the yeast and sugar with 4 tablespoons of tepid water and 1 tablespoon of the flour. Leave the blend in a warm place for 10 to 15 minutes until it is frothy.

Mix the remaining flour, the salt and the spices in a bowl. Add the melted butter, beaten eggs, chopped stem ginger, apricots and yeast blend, and beat the batter with a wooden spoon until the ingredients have combined evenly. Cover the batter with oiled plastic film and leave it in a warm place for 1 to 2 hours, until it has doubled in volume.

Generously butter a 20 cm (8 inch) kugelhopf mould. Stir the risen batter quickly, then spoon it into the prepared mould. Cover it with oiled

plastic film and leave it to rise again until it almost reaches the top of the mould – 45 minutes to 1 hour. Meanwhile, preheat the oven to 200°C (400°F or Mark 6).

Remove the plastic film and bake the kugelhopf for about 30 minutes, until golden-brown and firm to the touch. Leave it in the mould for 30 minutes, then turn it out on to a wire rack. When the cake is almost cold, melt the chocolate in a bowl over a saucepan of hot, but not boiling water, water and dribble it on to the cake from a spoon or a greaseproof paper piping bag. Sprinkle the cake with pine-nuts. Serve it when the chocolate has set.

# Steamed Malt Loaf

Serves 12

Working time: about 15 minutes

Total time: about 4 hours

Calories 205
Protein 4g
Cholesterol 0mg
Total fat 1g
Saturated fat 0g
Sodium 60mg

| 200 g | malt extract | 7 oz |
|---|---|---|
| 150 g | wholemeal flour | 5 oz |
| 150 g | rye flour | 5 oz |
| 150 g | cornmeal | 5 oz |

| 1½ tsp | baking powder | 1½ tsp |
|---|---|---|
| 45 cl | buttermilk | ¾ pint |
| 150 g | raisins | 5 oz |
| 90 g | molasses or black treacle | 3 oz |

Grease and flour a 25 by 10 cm (10 by 4 inch) loaf tin.

To make the cake, reserve 2 tablespoons of the malt extract for glazing, and stir the remaining malt extract well with all the other ingredients. Pour the batter into the prepared tin and level the surface. Cover the tin loosely with greased foil and set it on a trivet in a fish kettle or large fireproof casserole. Pour boiling water into the fish kettle to come half way up the sides of the loaf tin. Put a lid on the kettle, set it on the stove and adjust the heat so that the water simmers. Cook the loaf for about 2 hours, until it is risen and firm to the touch. Leave it in the tin for 10 minutes.

Turn the malt loaf on to a wire rack. Brush the loaf with the remaining malt extract while still warm, then leave the loaf to cool.

# Vinegar Cake

Serves 20

Working time: about 20 minutes

Total time: about 3 hours and 30 minutes

Calories 220

Protein 2g

Cholesterol 0mg

Total fat 8g

Saturated fat 2g

Sodium 130mg

| | | | | | | |
|---|---|---|---|---|---|---|
| 350 g | plain flour | 12 oz | | 125 g | mixed candied peel | 4 oz |
| 125 g | ground rice | 4 oz | | 17.5 cl | milk | 6 fl oz |
| ½ tsp | allspice | ½ tsp | | 3 tbsp | cider vineger | 3 tbsp |
| 175 g | polyunsaturated margarine | 6 oz | | 1 tsp | bicarbonate of soda | 1 tsp |
| 125 g | raisins | 4 oz | | 90 g | icing sugar | 3 oz |
| 125 g | sultanas | 4 oz | | 1½ tbsp | fresh lemon juice | 1½ tbsp |

Preheat the oven to 170°C (325°F or Mark 3). Grease a deep 25 by 11 cm (10 by 4½ inch) oblong tin. Line it with greaseproof paper and grease the paper.

Put the flour, ground rice and allspice into a mixing bowl. Add the margarine and rub it in finely with your fingertips until the mixture resembles breadcrumbs. Stir in the raisins, sultanas and candied peel.

Heat the milk in a saucepan until it is tepid. Stir in the vinegar and bicarbonate of soda, which will froth up. Immediately add the frothy liquid to the fruit mixture in the bowl, so as not to lose too much of the gas. Stir with a wooden spoon to blend the ingredients, then beat them to achieve a smooth, soft consistency. Spoon the

mixture into the prepared tin. Level the top with a small palette knife.

Bake the cake in the centre of the oven until well risen, golden-brown and springy when touched in the centre – about 1 hour and 10 minutes. Loosen the edges with a small palette knife, turn the cake out of the tin on to a wire rack and remove the lining paper. Leave the cake until it has cooled completely.

With a wooden spoon, beat the icing sugar with the lemon juice in a small bowl until smooth. Spoon the icing into a greaseproof paper piping bag and pipe a lattice design over the top of the cake. Leave the cake until the icing has set.

# Apricot and Orange Loaf

**Serves 16**

**Working time: about 30 minutes**

**Total time: about 4 hours and 30 minutes**

**Calories 175**

**Protein 7g**

**Cholesterol 40mg**

**Total fat 7g**

**Saturated fat 3g**

**Sodium 65mg**

| | | | | | | |
|---|---|---|---|---|---|---|
| **125 g** | dried apricots, chopped | **4 oz** | | **ɒʋ g** | light brown sugar | **2 oz** |
| **175 g** | sultanas | **6 oz** | | **2** | eggs, beaten | **2** |
| **15 cl** | fresh orange juice | **¼ pint** | | | | |
| **1 tsp** | finely grated orange rind | **1 tsp** | | | **Apricot-Walnut Topping** | |
| **60 g** | unsalted butter | **2 oz** | | **1 tbsp** | clear honey | **1 tbsp** |
| **175 g** | soya flour | **6 oz** | | **2 tbsp** | fresh orange juice | **2 tbsp** |
| **2 tsp** | baking powder | **2 tsp** | | **30 g** | shelled walnuts, chopped | **1 oz** |
| **60 g** | shelled walnuts, chopped | **2 oz** | | **6** | dried apricots, chopped | **6** |

Preheat the oven to 170°C (325°F or Mark 3). Grease a 22 by 11 cm (9 by 4½ inch) loaf tin. Line the base and the two long sides of the tin with greaseproof paper and grease the paper. Put the apricots, sultanas, orange juice, orange rind and butter in a pan. Heat gently, stirring occasionally, until the butter has melted; remove the pan from the heat.

Sift the soya flour and baking powder into a bowl. Mix in the walnuts and sugar. With a wooden spoon, stir in the eggs and the butter-fruit mixture from the saucepan, then beat until smooth and glossy.

Spoon the mixture into the prepared tin and level the top with a small palette knife. Bake the loaf in the centre of the oven until risen, lightly browned and springy when touched in the centre – about 1¼ hours. Loosen the edges with a small palette knife, turn the loaf out on to a wire rack and remove the lining paper. Leave the loaf until it is completely cold.

To make the topping, warm the honey and orange juice in a small saucepan. Boil them for 30 seconds, stirring occasionally. Put the walnuts in a small bowl and stir in half of the honey liquid. Add apricots to the liquid remaining in the pan and heat gently for 1 minute. Arrange walnuts in a band down the centre of the cake and spread the apricots on either side. Leave for a few minutes to let the topping cool and set.

# Fig Cake Encased in Shortcrust

**Serves 10**

Working time: about 45 minutes

Total time: about 3 hours and 30 minutes

Calories 230

Protein 5g

Cholesterol 50mg

Total fat 11g

Saturated fat 5g

Sodium 120mg

| | | |
|---|---|---|
| 125 g | dried figs, chopped | 4 oz |
| 125 g | dried pears, chopped | 4 oz |
| 60 g | dried dates, chopped | 2 oz |
| 30 g | unsalted butter, diced | 1 oz |
| 2 tbsp | Armagnac | 2 tbsp |
| 60 g | shelled walnuts, chopped | 2 oz |
| 1 | egg, beaten | 1 |
| 30 g | plain flour | 1 oz |

| | | |
|---|---|---|
| ½ tsp | ground cinnamon | ½ tsp |
| ¼ tsp | ground cloves | ¼ tsp |
| ⅛ tsp | salt | ⅛ tsp |
| | icing sugar to decorate | |
| | **Pastry Crust** | |
| 125 g | plain flour | 4 oz |
| 60 g | unsalted butter | 2 oz |
| | beaten egg white to glaze | |

Simmer figs, pears and dates in a saucepan with 6 tablespoons of water. Simmer gently until fruits are soft and water has been absorbed – 7 to 8 minutes. Add butter to pan and stir the mixture until the butter has melted. Let the mixture cool, then beat in the Armagnac, walnuts, eg, flour, cinnamon, cloves and salt. Set aside.

Preheat the oven to 180°C (350°F or Mark 4).

To make pastry, sift flour into a bowl. Rub in butter and mix in 4 teaspoons of iced water to make a firm dough. Roll out two thirds of the pastry on a lightly floured surface to make a rectangle large enough to cover base and sides of a 20 by 10 cm (8 by 4 inch) loaf tin. Press pastry against base and sides of tin evenly.

Spoon the filling into the tin and level the surface. Trim the pastry level with the top of the tin, then fold the pastry walls in over the filling. Add the trimmings to the reserved pastry and roll it out to make a rectangle to fit the top of the cake exactly. Trim the edges of the pastry lid, brush with egg white and lay it, brushed side down, on the filling. Press the edge well so that it sticks to the overlapping pastry walls. Using a fork, make a criss-cross pattern and decorative border on pastry lid. Brush lid with egg white.

Bake cake for 40 to 45 minutes, until pastry is pale golden. Let cake stand in tin for 10 minutes, then transfer it to a wire rack and leave it to cool. Dust the cake with icing sugar before serving.

22

# Tropical Fruit Cake

**Serves 24**

**Working time: about 30 minutes**

**Total time: about 5 hours**

Calories **275**
Protein **4g**
Cholesterol **45mg**
Total fat **10g**
Saturated fat **3g**
Sodium **145mg**

| | | |
|---|---|---|
| **250 g** | polyunsaturated margarine | **8 oz** |
| **250 g** | light brown sugar | **8 oz** |
| **4** | eggs | **4** |
| **350 g** | plain flour | **12 oz** |
| **3 tsp** | baking powder | **3 tsp** |
| **45 g** | angelica, chopped | **1½ oz** |

| | | |
|---|---|---|
| **125 g** | dried papaya, chopped | **4 oz** |
| **125 g** | dried pineapple, chopped | **4 oz** |
| **75 g** | shredded coconut | **2½ oz** |
| **60 g** | banana chips, crushed | **2 oz** |
| **2 tbsp** | skimmed milk | **2 tbsp** |
| **1 tbsp** | apricot jam without added sugar | **1 tbsp** |

Preheat the oven to 180°C (350°F or Mark 4). Grease a 22 cm (9 inch) round cake tin and line it with non-stick parchment paper.

Put the margarine, sugar and eggs in a mixing bowl. Sift in the flour and baking powder. Reserve 15 g (1½ oz) of the angelica, 30 g (1 oz) of the dried papaya, 30 g (1 oz) of the dried pineapple and 15 g (½ oz) of the shredded coconut for decoration. Roughly chop the rest of the shredded coconut. Add the remaining angelica, papaya, pineapple and chopped coconut to the bowl, then add the banana chips and the skimmed milk. Mix until the ingredients

are thoroughly blended, then beat the batter firmly with a wooden spoon for 2 minutes until it is smooth. Turn it into the prepared tin and level the top.

Cook the fruit cake for about 2 hours, until it is well browned and firm to the touch; a skewer inserted in the centre should come out clean.

Cool the cake for 5 minutes in the tin, then turn it out on to a wire rack and leave it to cool completely. Peel off the lining paper. Warm the jam in a small saucepan and brush it over the top of the cake. Sprinkle the top of the cake with the reserved tropical fruits.

# Stollen

Serves 24

Working
time: about
40 minutes

Total time:
about
7 hours

Calories
135

Protein
3g

Cholesterol
20mg

Total fat
4g

Saturated fat
2g

Sodium
15mg

| | | | | | |
|---|---|---|---|---|---|
| **30 g** | fresh yeast or 15 g (½ oz) dried yeast | **1 oz** | **1** | egg, beaten | **1** |
| **60 g** | vanilla-flavoured caster sugar | **2 oz** | **60 g** | raisins | **2 oz** |
| **6 tbsp** | skimmed milk | **6 tbsp** | **60 g** | currants | **2 oz** |
| **2 tbsp** | dark rum | **2 tbsp** | **60 g** | mixed candied peel, chopped | **2 oz** |
| **400 g** | plain flour | **14 oz** | **30 g** | glacé cherries, chopped | **1 oz** |
| **100 g** | unsalted butter | **3½ oz** | **30 g** | angelica, chopped | **1 oz** |
| | | | **2 tbsp** | icing sugar | **2 tbsp** |

In a bowl, blend yeast with 2 tablespoons of warm water. If using dried yeast, follow manufacturers instructions.

Warm skimmed milk in a pan. Remove pan from heat and dissolve sugar in the milk; add rum and yeast liquid. Sift flour into a large bowl and make a well in the centre. Cut 90 g (3 oz) of butter into bean-sized pieces and add to the flour. Add yeast mixture and beaten egg, raisins, currants, mixed peel, cherries and angelica. Mix ingredients and knead dough for 10 mins on a lightly floured surface or for 4 to 5 mins in an electric mixer.

Place dough in floured bowl, cover with oiled plastic film, and leave to rise in a warm place until doubled in size – about 2 hours. Knead until smooth. On a floured surface, roll dough out into a rectangle approximately 30 by 20 cm (12 by 8 inches). Fold one long side of rectangle over just beyond centre, fold the other long side to overlap first. Press down lightly to secure flap in position and move cake on to a well-greased baking sheet. Melt remaining butter and brush it over the surface of the stollen. Put the cake in a warm place for 20 to 30 minutes, until it has almost doubled in size. Meanwhile, preheat the oven to 190°C (375°F or Mark 5).

Cook the stollen for about 40 minutes, until it is well risen, browned and hollow-sounding when tapped on its base. Cool on a wire rack and dredge with icing sugar before serving.

# Dundee Cake

Serves 28

Working time: about 20 minutes

Total time: about 7 hours

Calories 215

Protein 3g

Cholesterol 40mg

Total fat 8g

Saturated fat 2g

Sodium 95mg

| | | | | | | |
|---|---|---|---|---|---|---|
| 250 g | currants | 8 oz | 90 g | medium oatmeal | 3 oz |
| 250 g | sultanas | 8 oz | 2 tsp | ground mixed spice | 2 tsp |
| 250 g | raisins | 8 oz | 125 g | light brown sugar | 4 oz |
| 60 g | mixed candied peel, chopped | 2 oz | 2 tbsp | molasses | 2 tbsp |
| 60 g | glacé cherries, quartered | 2 oz | 175 g | polyunsaturated margarine | 6 oz |
| 1 | orange, grated rind and juice | 1 | 4 | eggs, beaten | 4 |
| 250 g | wholemeal flour | 8 oz | 60 g | blanched almonds | 2 oz |
| 1 tsp | baking powder | 1 tsp | | | |

Preheat the oven to 140°C (275°F or Mark 1). Grease a deep, 18 cm (7 inch) square cake tin and double-line it with greaseproof paper. Grease the paper. To prevent the sides and base of the cake from scorching during the long cooking, tie a double thickness of brown paper round the outside of the tin and stand the tin on a baking sheet double-lined with brown paper.

Stir the currants, sultanas, raisins, mixed peel, glacé cherries, orange rind and juice together in a mixing bowl. Sift the flour and baking powder together in another bowl, adding the bran left in the sieve. Mix in the oatmeal, mixed spice, sugar, molasses, margarine and eggs. Beat the

mixture with a wooden spoon for 2 to 3 minutes until smooth and glossy.

Stir fruit into the cake batter. Spoon batter into the cake tin and level the top with a small palette knife. Arrange the almonds in rows on the cake.

Bake the cake in the centre of the oven until risen and dark brown – 2½ to 3 hours. Test the cake by inserting a warm skewer or cocktail stick into the centre of the cake. If it is clean when removed, the cake is cooked; otherwise return the cake to the oven and test it at 15-minute intervals.

Leave the cake to cool in the tin, then turn it out and remove the lining paper.

# Coffee Walnut Cake

| | | |
|---|---|---|
| Serves 14 | | Calories 210 |
| Working time: about 20 minutes | | Protein 4g |
| Total time: about 2 hours and 30 minutes | | Cholesterol 30mg |
| | | Total fat 13g |
| | | Saturated fat 2g |
| | | Sodium 185mg |

| | | | | | |
|---|---|---|---|---|---|
| 125 g | polyunsaturated margarine | 4 oz | 250 g | brown flour | 8 oz |
| 60 g | light brown sugar | 2 oz | 3 tsp | baking powder | 3 tsp |
| 4 tbsp | clear honey | 4 tbsp | 90 g | shelled walnuts, roughly chopped | 3 oz |
| 2 | eggs, beaten | 2 | | | |
| 2 tbsp | strong black coffee, cooled | 2 tbsp | 10 | shelled walnut halves | 10 |

Preheat the oven to 170°C (325°F or Mark 3). Grease a deep 20 cm (8 inch) round cake tin. Line it with greaseproof paper and grease the paper.

Put the margarine, sugar and honey into a mixing bowl. Beat them together with a wooden spoon until light and fluffy. Add the beaten egg a little at a time, beating well after each addition. Beat in the coffee.

Sift the brown flour and baking powder into the batter. Using a spatula or large metal spoon, fold the flour into the batter, then mix in the chopped walnuts. Spoon the cake mixture into the prepared tin. Level the top with a small palette knife and arrange the walnut halves round the edge.

Bake the cake in the centre of the oven until risen, lightly browned and springy when touched in the centre – 50 to 55 minutes. Loosen the edges of the cake with a small palette knife, turn it out on to a wire rack and remove the greaseproof paper. Leave the cake to cool before serving.

# Raisin and Ginger Buttermilk Cake

Serves 16

Working time: about 30 minutes

Total time: about 5 hours

Calories 220

Protein 3g

Cholesterol 0mg

Total fat 8g

Saturated fat 2g

Sodium 130mg

| | | | | | | |
|---|---|---|---|---|---|---|
| 175 g | plain flour | 6 oz | 1 | lemon, grated rind only | 1 |
| 175 g | wholemeal flour | 6 oz | 90 g | currants | 3 oz |
| ½ tsp | ground cinnamon | ½ tsp | 90 g | raisins | 3 oz |
| ¼ tsp | ground ginger | ¼ tsp | 60 g | mixed candied peel, chopped | 2 oz |
| ¼ tsp | ground mixed spice | ¼ tsp | ¼ litre | buttermilk | 8 fl oz |
| 150 g | polyunsaturated margarine | 5 oz | 1 tbsp | black treacle | 1 tbsp |
| 125 g | light brown sugar | 4 oz | ¾ tsp | bicarbonate of soda | ¾ tsp |

Preheat the oven to 170°C (325°F or Mark 3). Line a 22 by 12 cm (9 by 5 inch) loaf tin with non-stick parchment paper.

Sift the plain flour into a bowl and mix in the wholemeal flour, cinnamon, ginger and mixed spice. Add the margarine and rub it in until the mixture resembles fine breadcrumbs. Mix in the sugar, lemon rind, currants, raisins and peel. Heat the buttermilk gently in a saucepan, then stir in the treacle until it melts. Add the bicarbonate

of soda to the pan and stir until it froths. Combine this liquid with the dry ingredients and mix until they are evenly blended.

Turn the mixture into the prepared tin and level the top. Cook the buttermilk cake for about 1¼ hours, until it is well risen and firm to the touch; a skewer inserted in the centre should come out clean. Turn the buttermilk cake out on to a wire rack and leave it to cool completely before removing the lining paper.

# Banana Tofu Cake

**Serves 10**

**Working time: about 30 minutes**

**Total time: about 3 hours**

Calories 290

Protein 20g

Cholesterol 20mg

Total fat 10g

Saturated fat 4g

Sodium 35mg

| | | |
|---|---|---|
| **175 g** | stoned fresh dates, chopped | **6 oz** |
| **30 cl** | fresh orange juice | **½ pint** |
| **175 g** | peeled bananas, sliced | **6 oz** |
| **500 g** | tofu | **1 lb** |
| **1 tbsp** | agar flakes | **1 tbsp** |
| **1 tsp** | finely grated lemon rind | **1 tsp** |
| **½ tsp** | ground mixed spice | **½ tsp** |
| **1 tbsp** | apricot jam without added sugar | **1 tbsp** |

| | | |
|---|---|---|
| **1 tbsp** | finely chopped skinned toasted hazelnuts | **1 tbsp** |
| | **Spicy Oat Base** | |
| **125 g** | wholemeal flour | **4 oz** |
| **125 g** | rolled oats | **4 oz** |
| **75 g** | unsalted butter, melted | **2½ oz** |
| **30 g** | malt extract | **1 oz** |
| **1 tsp** | ground mixed spice | **1 tsp** |

Preheat the oven to 180°C (350°F or Mark 4). To make the spicy oat base, combine the flour, oats, butter, malt extract and mixed spice in a bowl. Press them into the bottom of a 20 cm (8 inch) springform tin. Bake the base for 15 minutes, then leave it to cool.

Simmer the dates in the orange juice for about 12 minutes, until the dates are very soft. Put the dates and juice in a food processor or blender together with the bananas, tofu, agar flakes, lemon rind and mixed spice. Blend to a purée. Spoon the purée over the oat base and level the surface. Bake the cake for 40 to 45 minutes, until it is firm when pressed in the centre. Leave the cake to cool in the tin.

While the cake is cooling, heat the apricot jam in a small saucepan. Sieve the jam into a bowl and brush it over the surface of the cake. Sprinkle the chopped hazelnuts round the edge of the cake.

*Editor's Note:* Two large peeled bananas weigh about 175 g (6 oz). Four large oranges yield about 30 cl (½ pint) of juice. To toast and skin hazelnuts, place them on a baking sheet in a 180°C (350°F or Mark 4) oven for 10 minutes. Enfold the nuts in a towel and loosen the skins by rubbing briskly.

# Pineapple Cake

**Serves 12**

Working
time: about
25 minutes

Total time:
about
3 hours

Calories
220
Protein
4g
Cholesterol
40mg
Total fat
10g
Saturated fat
2g
Sodium
95mg

| 125 g | polyunsaturated margarine | 4 oz | 1¾ tsp | baking powder | 1¾ tsp |
| 125 g | light brown sugar | 4 oz | 125 g | currants | 4 oz |
| 2 | eggs | 2 | 200 g | fresh pineapple flesh | 7 oz |
| 200 g | plain flour | 7 oz | | | |

Preheat the oven to 170°C (325°F or Mark 3). Line a 20 cm (8 inch) round cake tin with greaseproof paper and grease the paper.

Using a wooden spoon, cream the margarine and sugar together until light and fluffy. Beat in the eggs one at a time, following each with 1 tablespoon of the flour. Sift in the remaining flour, together with the baking powder. With a metal spoon or rubber spatula, fold the flour into the batter, then mix in the currants. Purée the pineapple in a food processor or blender, and fold it into the cake mixture.

Turn the mixture into the prepared tin and level the top. Bake the pineapple cake for about 1¼ hours, until it is firm to the touch and golden-brown. Leave the cake in the tin for 10 minutes, then turn it on to a wire rack and leave it to cool. Remove the lining paper.

*Suggested accompaniment:* sliced fresh pineapple

# Banana Layer Cake

Serves 12

Working time: about 30 minutes

Total time: about 2 hours

Calories
235
Protein
5g
Cholesterol
45mg
Total fat
11g
Saturated fat
2g
Sodium
70mg

| 90 g | soft brown sugar | 3 oz |
|------|------------------|------|
| 10 cl | safflower oil | 3½ fl oz |
| 2 | eggs | 2 |
| 3 | bananas, peeled and mashed | 3 |
| 1 tsp | finely grated lemon rind | 1 tsp |
| 175 g | wholemeal flour | 6 oz |
| 1½ tsp | baking powder | 1½ tsp |
| ¼ tsp | ground allspice | ¼ tsp |

| 60 g | rolled oats | 2 oz |
|------|-------------|------|
| ½ tsp | icing sugar | ½ tsp |
| | **Yogurt-Banana Filling** | |
| 175 g | thick Greek yogurt | 6 oz |
| 1 | banana, peel and finely chopped | 1 |

Preheat the oven to 180°C (350°F or Mark 4). Grease a 22 by 18 cm (9 by 7 inch) cake tin; line the base with greaseproof paper and grease the paper.

Whisk together the brown sugar, oil and eggs until thick and pale. Stir in the mashed bananas and lemon rind. Sift the flour with the baking powder and allspice into the banana mixture, adding the bran left in the sieve. Add the oats and then fold the ingredients together with a metal spoon. Transfer the batter to the prepared

tin and level the surface. Bake the banana cake for about 30 minutes, until risen and firm to the touch. Leave it in the tin for 10 minutes, then transfer it to a wire tray to cool.

Remove the paper and trim the edges. Split the cake in half horizontally and halve each piece again.

To make the filling, mix the yogurt with the chopped banana. Sandwich the four layers of cake together with the banana mixture and dust the top of the cake with the icing sugar.

# Apple and Date Cake

Serves 14

Working
time: about
20 minutes

Total time:
about
4 hours

Calories
240
Protein
5g
Cholesterol
50mg
Total fat
7g
Saturated fat
1g
Sodium
100mg

| | | | | | | |
|---|---|---|---|---|---|---|
| 300 g | wholemeal flour | 10 oz | 500 g | dessert apples, peeled and | 1 lb |
| 3 tsp | baking powder | 3 tsp | | cored | |
| 2 tsp | ground mixed spice | 2 tsp | 15 cl | medium-sweet cider | ¼ pint |
| ½ tsp | grated nutmeg | ½ tsp | 3 | eggs | 3 |
| 125 g | dark brown sugar | 4 oz | 8 cl | safflower oil | 3 fl oz |
| 250 g | dried dates, chopped | 8 oz | 2 tbsp | clear honey | 2 tbsp |

Preheat the oven to 180°C (350°F or Mark 4). Grease a deep, 20 cm (8 inch) round cake tin. Line the base with greaseproof paper and grease the paper.

Sift the flour and baking powder into a bowl, adding the bran left in the sieve. Stir in the mixed spice, nutmeg, sugar and dates. Grate half the apples and add them to the dry ingredients with the cider, eggs and oil. With a wooden spoon, beat the ingredients together thoroughly and turn them into the prepared tin.

Slice the remaining apples thinly and overlap the slices in two circles on top of the cake; stand a few slices upright in the centre. Bake for 1¼ to 1½ hours, until a skewer inserted in the centre comes out clean.

Turn the cake on to a wire rack and remove the lining paper. While the cake is still warm, boil the honey for 1 minute in a small saucepan. Brush the apples with the honey, then leave the cake to cool.

# Courgette Cake

Serves 12

Working time: about 15 minutes

Total time: about 2 hours and 30 minutes

Calories 225

Protein 4g

Cholesterol 25mg

Total fat 9g

Saturated fat 3g

Sodium 155mg

| | | |
|---|---|---|
| 250 g | courgettes, coarsely grated | 8 oz |
| 125 g | fresh dates, stoned and chopped | 4 oz |
| 60 g | raisins | 2 oz |
| 4 tbsp | clear honey | 4 tbsp |
| 125 g | polyunsaturated margarine | 4 oz |
| 125 g | light brown sugar | 4 oz |
| 1 | egg, beaten | 1 |
| 250 g | brown flour | 8 oz |
| 2 tsp | baking powder | 2 tsp |

Preheat the oven to 170°C (325°F or Mark 3). Grease a shallow 22 cm (9 inch) cake tin. Line its base with greaseproof paper and grease the paper.

Stir the courgettes with the dates, raisins and honey in a mixing bowl. In another bowl, cream the margarine and sugar together until light and fluffy. Add the eggs with 2 tablespoons of water, and beat with a wooden spoon until the mixture is smooth and glossy.

Sift the flour with the baking powder, and fold them into the creamed margarine mixture using a spatula or large spoon. Then fold in the courgettes, dates and raisins. Spoon the mixture into the prepared tin and level the top with a small palette knife. Bake the courgette cake in the centre of the oven until risen, lightly browned and springy when touched in the centre – 55 to 60 minutes.

Loosen the cake from the sides of the tin with a small palette knife. Turn the cake on to a wire rack and remove the lining paper. Leave the cake until it has cooled completely before serving.

# Pumpkin Cake

Serves 16

Working time: about 20 minutes

Total time: about 3 hours

Calories 170
Protein 4g
Cholesterol 15mg
Total fat 9g
Saturated fat 3g
Sodium 180mg

| | | |
|---|---|---|
| **500 g** | pumpkin, peeled and chopped | **1 lb** |
| **175 g** | brown flour | **6 oz** |
| **3 tsp** | baking powder | **3 tsp** |
| **1 tsp** | ground cinnamon | **1 tsp** |
| **125 g** | medium oatmeal | **4 oz** |
| **60 g** | light brown sugar | **2 oz** |
| **90 g** | polyunsaturated margarine | **3 oz** |

| | | |
|---|---|---|
| **1** | egg, beaten | **1** |
| | **Honey-Cheese Topping** | |
| **250 g** | medium-fat curd cheese | **8 oz** |
| **2 tbsp** | plain low-fat yogurt | **2 tbsp** |
| **4 tsp** | clear honey | **4 tsp** |
| **2 tbsp** | pumpkin seeds, lightly browned | **2 tbsp** |

Preheat the oven to 170°C (325°F or Mark 3). Grease an 18 cm (7 inch) square cake tin. Line the tin with greaseproof paper and grease the paper.

Put the pumpkin in a pan with 4 tablespoons of water. Simmer for 2 to 3 minutes, or until the pumpkin is tender. Strain the pumpkin and purée it in a blender or food processor. You should have at least ¼ litre (8 fl oz) of purée. Leave it to cool.

Sift the flour into a bowl with the baking powder and cinnamon. Add the oatmeal and brown sugar, and stir. Rub in the margarine with the fingertips until the mixture resembles breadcrumbs.

Stir in the egg and ¼ litre (8 fl oz) of the pumpkin purée, then beat the mixture with a wooden spoon for 1 minute until smooth. Spoon the mixture into the tin and level the top.

Bake the cake in the centre of the oven until risen, golden-brown and springy when touched in the centre – 50 to 60 minutes. Turn the cake on to a wire rack and remove the paper. Leave to cool completely.

Meanwhile, make the topping. Put the curd cheese, yogurt and honey in a bowl and mix them together with a wooden spoon. Spread the top and sides of the cake evenly with the topping and score it with a fork. Press pumpkin seeds against the sides of the cake.

# Parsnip and Orange Cake

Serves 14

Working time: about 30 minutes

Total time: about 4 hours

Calories 210

Protein 5g

Cholesterol 40mg

Total fat 10g

Saturated fat 2g

Sodium 240mg

| | | |
|---|---|---|
| **125 g** | polyunsaturated margarine | **4 oz** |
| **125 g** | brown sugar | **4 oz** |
| **2 tbsp** | malt extract | **2 tbsp** |
| **1** | orange, grated rind and juice only | **1** |
| **3** | eggs | **3** |
| **275 g** | wholemeal flour | **9 oz** |
| **1 tbsp** | baking powder | **1 tbsp** |
| **250 g** | parsnips, peeled and grated | **8 oz** |

**Orange Topping**

| | | |
|---|---|---|
| **90 g** | medium-fat curd cheese | **3 oz** |
| **2 tsp** | clear honey | **2 tsp** |
| **1** | orange, rind only, half grated, half julienned and blanched | **1** |

Preheat the oven to 170°C (325°F or Mark 3). Grease a deep 20 cm (8 inch) round cake tin. Line the base with greaseproof paper and grease the paper.

Cream the margarine, sugar, malt extract and orange rind until fluffy. Beat in the eggs one at a time, adding 1 tablespoon of flour with each egg. Sift the remaining flour with the baking powder, adding the bran left in the sieve. Fold the flour, parsnips and orange juice into the batter.

Turn the batter into the prepared tin. Bake the cake for about 1¼ hours, until a skewer inserted into the centre comes out clean.

Loosen the cake from the sides of the tin; turn the cake out on to a wire rack and remove the lining paper. Turn the cake the right way up and leave it to cool completely before icing it.

To make the orange topping, beat the curd cheese, honey and grated orange rind together. Spread the mixture over the top of the cake and flute it with a palette knife. Sprinkle the orange julienne round the edge of the cake.

# Banana Walnut Cake

Makes 14

Working
time: about
40 minutes

Total time:
about
4 hours

Calories
285
Protein
4g
Cholesterol
25mg
Total fat
15g
Saturated fat
3g
Sodium
125mg

| | | | | | | |
|---|---|---|---|---|---|---|
| 125 g | plain flour | 4 oz | | 8 cl | safflower oil | 3 fl oz |
| 4 tsp | baking powder | 4 tsp | | | **Lemon Butter Icing** | |
| 125 g | wholemeal flour | 4 oz | | 45 g | unsalted butter | 1½ oz |
| 150 g | light brown sugar | 5 oz | | 45 g | medium-fat curd cheese | 1½ oz |
| 75 g | shelled walnuts | 2½ oz | | ¼ tsp | grated lemon rind | ¼ tsp |
| 125 g | carrots, finely grated | 4 oz | | 90 g | icing sugar | 3 oz |
| 175 g | peeled bananas, mashed | 6 oz | | | | |
| 1 | egg | 1 | | | | |

Preheat the oven to 180°C (350°F or Mark 4). Line an 18 cm (7 inch) square cake tin with non-stick parchment paper.

Sift the plain flour and baking powder into a bowl and mix in the wholemeal flour and brown sugar. Finely chop 45 g (1½ oz) of the walnuts and stir them in, together with the carrots. Using a wooden spoon, beat the mashed bananas with the egg and oil in a separate bowl. Make a well in the centre of the dry ingredients, add the banana mixture and beat the batter until it is smooth.

Turn the batter into the tin, level the top and cook the cake for about 1 hour, until a skewer inserted in the centre comes out clean. Turn the cake out on to a wire rack and leave it to cool with the paper still attached.

To make the lemon butter icing, beat the butter with a wooden spoon until soft, then beat in the curd cheese and lemon rind. Sift in enough icing sugar to give a spreading consistency. Remove the paper from the cake and turn the cake the right way up. Spread the icing over the top of the cake, swirling it with a round-bladed knife. Break the remaining walnuts into large pieces and sprinkle over the icing.

*Editor's Note:* Two bananas weigh approximately 175 g (6 oz) when peeled.

# Strawberry Ring

Serves 14

Working time: about 30 minutes

Total time: about 2 hours

Calories 120

Protein 2g

Cholesterol 0mg

Total fat 3g

Saturated fat 0g

Sodium 65mg

| 125 g | plain flour | 4 oz |
|---|---|---|
| 2 tsp | baking powder | 2 tsp |
| 60 g | ground rice | 2 oz |
| 90 g | caster sugar | 3 oz |
| 1 tsp | pure vanilla extract | 1 tsp |
| 3 tbsp | safflower oil | 3 tbsp |

| 4 | egg whites | 4 |
|---|---|---|
| 250 g | strawberries, hulled | 8 oz |
| 1 tsp | arrowroot | 1 tsp |
| 30 g | icing sugar | 1 oz |
| | strawberry leaves to garnish | |

Preheat the oven to 180°C (350°F or Mark 4). Grease and lightly flour a 22 cm (9 inch) springform ring mould – preferably one with a pattern on its base.

Sift the flour and baking powder into a mixing bowl. Stir in the ground rice and caster sugar. In another bowl, whisk the vanilla extract with the oil and 4 tablespoons of water. Stir the liquids into the dry ingredients using a wooden spoon, then beat the mixture to a smooth batter.

Whisk the egg whites in a bowl until they are stiff but not dry. With a large metal or plastic spoon, fold one third of the egg whites into the batter, followed by the remaining egg whites.

Pour the mixture into the prepared mould. Tap the mould to level the mixture. Bake the cake in the centre of the oven until well risen and springy when touched in the centre – 20 to 25 minutes. Loosen the edges of the cake with a small palette knife, release the spring and turn the cake out on to a wire rack to cool completely.

Sieve four of the strawberries into a small saucepan. Blend the purée with the arrowroot, then sift in the icing sugar. Bring the purée to the boil, stirring, and simmer it for 30 seconds, until it thickens. Leave the purée to cool completely.

Thinly slice half of the remaining strawberries and arrange them on the inner edge of the cake. Fill the hole in the centre with the whole strawberries and top them with a few strawberry leaves. Brush the top and sides of the ring with the strawberry purée.

# Black Cherry Chocolate Gateau

Serves 12

Working time: about 50 minutes

Total time: about 3 hours

Calories 140

Protein 5g

Cholesterol 60mg

Total fat 5g

Saturated fat 3g

Sodium 80mg

| | | | | | | |
|---|---|---|---|---|---|---|
| **500 g** | black cherries | **1 lb** | **½ tsp** | baking powder | **½ tsp** | |
| **1½ tsp** | powdered gelatine | **1½ tsp** | **3 tbsp** | kirsch or brandy | **3 tbsp** | |
| **3** | eggs | **3** | **175 g** | medium-fat soft cheese | **6 oz** | |
| **100 g** | caster sugar | **3½ oz** | **5 tbsp** | whipping cream, whipped | **5 tbsp** | |
| **90 g** | plain flour | **3 oz** | **15 g** | chocolate curls | **½ oz** | |
| **15 g** | cocoa powder | **½ oz** | | | | |

Preheat oven to 190°C (375°F or Mark 5). Grease a round cake tin about 21 cm (8½ inches) in diameter and line with parchment paper.

Set aside 13 or 14 cherries to decorate cake. Simmer rest very gently in 15 cl (¼ pint) of water until tender but intact – 7 to 8 minutes. Strain liquid into a measuring jug and, if necessary, top up with water to 175 cl (6 fl oz). Put 1 tablespoon of water in a bowl, stand in a pan of simmering water. Add gelatine. When dissolved, stir into liquid. Halve the cherries, discard stones, and add to liquid. Cool then refrigerate until set – about 2 hours.

Put eggs and all but 2 teaspoons of sugar in a bowl over a pan of hot, but not boiling, water. Whisk until eggs are thick and pale. Remove bowl from the heat, whisking until whisk leaves a heavy trail when lifted. Sift flour, cocoa and baking powder together and fold evenly through egg mixture with a metal spoon. Turn the batter into the tin and level. Cook for 20 to 25 minutes, until well risen and firm to the touch. Turn the sponge out on to a wire rack; loosen the lining paper but do not remove and leave the sponge to cool.

Cut the sponge in half horizontally and place bottom half on a plate. Sprinkle with kirsch. Mix the cheese with remaining sugar and spread half of it over the sponge. Stir the cherry jelly, and spread it and the stewed cherries evenly over the cheese. Top with the second layer of sponge. Spread its top with the remaining cheese mixture.

Spoon the cream into a piping bag fitted with a small star nozzle. Pipe a lattice of cream on the cake, and garnish with chocolate curls and cherries.

# Piña Colada Gateau

| | | |
|---|---|---|
| Serves 12 | | |
| Working time: about 45 minutes | | |
| Total time: about 2 hours and 45 minutes | | |

| | | |
|---|---|---|
| Calories 235 | | |
| Protein 4g | | |
| Cholesterol 80mg | | |
| Total fat 13g | | |
| Saturated fat 9g | | |
| Sodium 130mg | | |

| | | |
|---|---|---|
| 90 g | unsalted butter | 3 oz |
| 90 g | caster sugar | 3 oz |
| 2 | eggs, lightly beaten | 2 |
| 90 g | plain flour | 3 oz |
| 1 tsp | baking powder | 1 tsp |
| 60 g | desiccated coconut | 2 oz |
| | **Pineapple and Rum Custard** | |
| 2 tbsp | plain flour | 2 tbsp |

| | | |
|---|---|---|
| 2 tbsp | cornflour | 2 tbsp |
| 30 g | caster sugar | 1 oz |
| 1 | egg yolk | 1 |
| 30 cl | skimmed milk | ½ pint |
| 125 g | fresh pineapple flesh, finely chopped | 4 oz |
| 1 tbsp | dark rum | 1 tbsp |
| 30 g | desiccated coconut | 1 oz |

Preheat oven to 180°C (350°F or Mark 4). Grease two 20 cm (8 inch) round sandwich tins. Line bases with greaseproof paper and grease paper.

Cream butter and sugar together in a bowl until pale and fluffy. Beat eggs into the creamed butter a little at a time. Sift flour and baking powder together into egg mixture, and add the desiccated coconut, folding in with a metal spoon.

Divide mixture equally between prepared tins; level the surfaces. Bake sponges for about 20 minutes, until risen and firm to the touch. Turn them out on to a wire rack to cool with the lining paper still attached.

Using a wooden spoon, mix together flour, cornflour, sugar and egg yolk with half of milk in a bowl. Bring remaining milk to the boil in a pan and pour over egg mixture, stirring well. Return custard to pan and cook over gentle heat, stirring, until thickened enough to leave a trail. Pour custard into a bowl to cool and cover it closely with plastic film to prevent a skin forming.

Pour half of the custard into a second bowl. Add the pineapple to one bowl and the rum to the other. Remove the lining paper from the sponges and sandwich them together with the pineapple custard. Coat the top and sides of the cake with the rum custard. Scatter desiccated coconut evenly over the rum custard.

# Cool Caribbean Cake

Serves 10

Working time: about 40 minutes

Total time: about 5 hours

Calories 180

Protein 4g

Cholesterol 5mg

Total fat 5g

Saturated fat 2g

Sodium 95mg

| | | |
|---|---|---|
| **60 g** | plain chocolate | **2 oz** |
| **2 tsp** | clear honey | **2 tsp** |
| **15 g** | unsalted butter | **½ oz** |
| **125 g** | breakfast wheat flakes | **4 oz** |
| **2 tbsp** | whipped cream | **2 tbsp** |
| **1 tbsp** | coconut flakes | **1 tbsp** |
| | **Coconut Ice Cream** | |
| **60 g** | creamed coconut | **2 oz** |
| **2 tbsp** | clear honey | **2 tbsp** |

| | | |
|---|---|---|
| **15 cl** | plain low-fat yogurt | **¼ pint** |
| **1** | egg white | **1** |
| | **Mango Ice Cream** | |
| **2** | mangoes, peeled and chopped | **2** |
| **4 tbsp** | fresh orange juice | **4 tbsp** |
| **2 tbsp** | clear honey | **2 tbsp** |
| **15 cl** | plain low-fat yogurt | **¼ pint** |
| **1** | egg white | **1** |

Line an 18 cm (7 inch) round cake tin with non-stick parchment paper. Put chocolate, honey and butter in a bowl over a pan of hot (not boiling) water, stirring until melted. Stir wheat flakes through chocolate mixture. Spread chocolate wheat flakes in the base of the tin. Level and press well down. Put the tin in the freezer.

Put 15 cl (¼ pint) of water in a small pan and bring to the boil. Remove from heat and stir in creamed coconut and honey. Leave to cool completely, then stir in the yogurt and pour the mixture into a shallow plastic container. Freeze the coconut ice cream until firm but not hard – about 1 hour.

Meanwhile, purée mangoes with orange juice, honey and yogurt. Pour into a shallow container and freeze until firm but not frozen hard – 1-2 hours.

To break down coconut ice cream crystals, whisk or blend until smooth. Whisk egg white until stiff in a separate bowl, then whisk into ice cream. Pour over chocolate layer and freeze the two layers until firm but not frozen hard.

Repeat procedure with mango ice-cream, then pour on top of frozen layers. Freeze for about 2 hours.

Dip the tin base in warm water to turn cake out onto a plate. Remove paper and decorate cake with piped cream and coconut flakes.

# Strawberry Shortcake

**Serves 10**

**Working time: about 45 minutes**

**Total time: about 2 hours and 30 minutes**

Calories
220

Protein
5g

Cholesterol
25mg

Total fat
11g

Saturated fat
4g

Sodium
305mg

| | | | |
|---|---|---|---|
| **150 g** | plain flour | **5 oz** | |
| **60 g** | ground almonds | **2 oz** | |
| **3 tbsp** | caster sugar | **3 tbsp** | |
| **1 tbsp** | baking powder | **1 tbsp** | |
| **45 g** | unsalted butter | **1½ oz** | |
| **5 tbsp** | buttermilk | **5 tbsp** | |
| **15 g** | flaked almonds | **½ oz** | |

**Strawberry Filling**

| | | |
|---|---|---|
| **250 g** | strawberries, one reserved, the rest hulled and chopped | **8 oz** |
| **4 tbsp** | claret or port | **4 tbsp** |
| **125 g** | cottage cheese, sieved | **4 oz** |
| **4 tbsp** | double cream, whipped | **4 tbsp** |
| **1 tbsp** | caster sugar | **1 tbsp** |
| | icing sugar to decorate | |

Preheat the oven to 200°C (400°F or Mark 6). Add the chopped strawberries for the filling to the claret and leave them to macerate.

Sift the flour, ground almonds, sugar and baking powder together into a bowl. Rub in the butter until the mixture resembles fine crumbs. Stir in about 4 tablespoons of the buttermilk – enough to give a soft dough. Knead the dough gently on a lightly floured surface, then press it out to an 18 cm (7 inch) round. Place the round on a non-stick baking sheet.

With a knife, mark the top of the dough into 10 sections. Brush the top with buttermilk and sprinkle it with the almonds. Bake the shortcake for about 25 minutes, until it is crisp and golden.

Turn it out to cool on a wire rack. When the shortcake is cold, split it in half horizontally and cut the top into the 10 sections.

To make the strawberry filling, mix the cottage cheese with the whipped cream and caster sugar. Strain the juice from the macerated strawberries and keep it for another use; then fold the strawberries into the cream mixture.

Just before serving the cake, spread the strawberry cream over the base of the shortcake. Cover it with the 10 top sections and dust them lightly with icing sugar. Slice the reserved strawberry and arrange the slices in the centre of the cake.

# Layered Marron and Orange Gateau

Serves 10

Working time: about 30 minutes

Total time: about 2 hours and 30 minutes

Calories 230

Protein 5g

Cholesterol 50mg

Total fat 7g

Saturated fat 2g

Sodium 100mg

| | | | | | |
|---|---|---|---|---|---|
| **125 g** | brown flour | **4 oz** | **1** | orange, skin and pith sliced off, flesh cut into segments | **1** |
| **1½ tsp** | baking powder | **1½ tsp** | | | |
| **90 g** | light brown sugar | **3 oz** | | **Orange Chestnut Filling** | |
| **2 tbsp** | safflower oil | **2 tbsp** | **450 g** | chestnut purée | **15 oz** |
| **2** | eggs, yolks and whites separated | **2** | **1** | orange, grated rind only | **1** |
| **1 tsp** | grated orange rind | **1 tsp** | **4 tbsp** | plain low-fat yogurt | **4 tbsp** |
| **45 g** | shelled hazelnuts, toasted and finely chopped | **1½ oz** | **1 tbsp** | clear honey | **1 tbsp** |

Preheat oven to 180°C (350°F or Mark 4). Grease a deep 20 cm (8 inch) cake tin and line base with greased and floured greaseproof paper.

Sift the flour and baking powder together into a mixing bowl and stir in the sugar. Whisk the oil in a bowl with the egg yolks, the orange rind and 3 tablespoons of water. Stir into the flour mixture, then beat with a wooden spoon to make a smooth, glossy batter. In another bowl, whisk the egg whites until stiff but not dry. Add one third of the whites to the batter and fold them in using a metal spoon. Fold in remaining whites and pour the mixture into the prepared tin. Tap the tin to level the mixture.

Bake the cake in the centre of the oven for 25 to 30 minutes, until well risen, lightly browned and springy to touch. Loosen edges of the cake with a palette knife and turn on to a wire rack. Remove paper and leave to cool completely.

To make filling, beat chestnut purée, orange rind, yogurt and honey in a bowl until smooth. Spoon 2 tablespoons of the filling into a piping bag fitted with a small star nozzle.

Cut cake into three layers. Put base layer on a plate and spread top surface with one quarter of the filling over the top sides of the cake. Press the hazelnuts against the sides of cake to coat them evenly. Arrange the orange segments radiating outwards from the centre. Pipe stars round top of the cake and a rosette in the centre.

# Pear and Port Wine Cheesecake

Serves 12

Working time: about 40 minutes

Total time: about 2 hours and 30 minutes

Calories 200

Protein 4g

Cholesterol 35mg

Total fat 10g

Saturated fat 3g

Sodium 195mg

| | | | | | |
|---|---|---|---|---|---|
| **175 g** | digestive biscuits, crushed | **6 oz** | **1** | egg | **1** |
| **60 g** | unsalted butter, melted | **2 oz** | **3** | large pears | **3** |
| **1 tsp** | ground cinnamon | **1 tsp** | **1 tbsp** | fresh lemon juice | **1 tbsp** |
| **250 g** | medium-fat curd cheese | **8 oz** | **6 tbsp** | port | **6 tbsp** |
| **60 g** | caster sugar | **2 oz** | **1 tbsp** | currants | **1 tbsp** |
| **1 tsp** | finely grated lemon rind | **1 tsp** | **1 tsp** | arrowroot | **1 tsp** |

Preheat the oven to 180°C (350°F or Mark 4). In a bowl, mix the biscuit crumbs with the butter and cinnamon. Spread the mixture over the bottom of a 22 cm (9 inch) round springform cake tin and press lightly. Bake the biscuit for 15 minutes, then leave it to cool.

With a wooden spoon, beat together the curd cheese, sugar, lemon rind and egg. Peel and core the pears. Slice them thinly and sprinkle the slices with lemon juice. Cover the biscuit base with the cheese mixture, then arrange the pear slices on top in an overlapping pattern. Bake the cheesecake for about 35 minutes until it is set. Leave the cake to cool in the tin, then transfer it to a serving plate.

Put the port, currants and arrowroot in a small pan. Cook them, stirring, over gentle heat for 1 minute, until the liquid thickens. Leave it for a minute or two to cool; spoon the mixture over the cake to glaze the pears.

# Redcurrant and Blackcurrant Cheesecake

<table>
<tr><td>Serves 12</td><td rowspan="2"></td><td>Calories<br>195</td></tr>
</table>

**Serves 12**

**Working time: about 30 minutes**

**Total time: about 3 hours**

**Calories**
195

**Protein**
7g

**Cholesterol**
30mg

**Total fat**
10g

**Saturated fat**
3g

**Sodium**
180mg

| | | |
|---|---|---:|
| **90 g** | brown flour | **3 oz** |
| **30 g** | wholemeal semolina | **1 oz** |
| **1 tsp** | baking powder | **1 tsp** |
| **45 g** | unsalted butter | **1½ oz** |
| **3 tbsp** | clear honey | **3 tbsp** |
| **500 g** | medium-fat curd cheese | **1 lb** |
| **15 cl** | plain low-fat yogurt | **¼ pint** |

| | | |
|---|---|---:|
| **1 tsp** | pure vanilla extract | **1 tsp** |
| **1** | egg | **1** |
| **250 g** | redcurrants, picked over, stemmed | **8 oz** |
| **250 g** | blackcurrants, picked over stemmed | **8 oz** |
| **60 g** | caster sugar | **2 oz** |
| **4 tsp** | arrowroot | **4 tsp** |

Preheat oven to 180°C (350°F or Mark 4). Grease an 18 cm (7 inch) loose-based square cake tin.

Sift brown flour, semolina and baking powder into a bowl. Rub in butter until mixture resembles breadcrumbs. Using a fork, stir in 1 tablespoon of honey and 2 teaspoons of cold water. Knead dough on a floured surface, roll it out and cut to fit cake tin. Lower dough into tin and press it well against the base and sides. Prick with a fork and bake for 10 minutes. Remove it from the oven and reduce the oven temperature to 150°C (300°F or Mark 2).

Beat the curd cheese, yogurt, remaining honey and vanilla extract in a bowl. Add egg and beat until smooth. Pour mixture into tin, bake until filling has

set – about 1 hour. Let cool in tin, transfer to a plate.

While cheesecake cooks, put redcurrants and blackcurrants in separate pans and split the caster sugar between pans. Cook currants gently for 2 minutes, shaking occasionally, until currants are soft but still whole. Strain contents of both pans; put redcurrants and blackcurrants in separate bowls and return each juice to its original pan.

Blend arrowroot with 2 tablespoons of water, stir half into each pan. Bring both pans of juice to the boil, stirring, cook for 1 minute. Stir the thickened redcurrant juice into the blackcurrants and the thickened blackcurrant juice into the redcurrants. Chill . Arrange bands of the currants on top of the cooled cheesecake.

# Muesli Cheese Tart

<table>
<tr><td>Serves 12</td><td rowspan="4"></td><td>Calories<br>170</td></tr>
<tr><td>Working<br>time: about<br>30 minutes</td><td>Protein<br>8g</td></tr>
<tr><td rowspan="2">Total time:<br>about<br>2 hours</td><td>Cholesterol<br>35mg</td></tr>
<tr><td>Total fat<br>8g</td></tr>
</table>

Saturated fat
3g

Sodium
80mg

| | | |
|---|---|---|
| **350 g** | low-fat soft cheese | **12 oz** |
| **1 tbsp** | clear honey | **1 tbsp** |
| **1** | egg | **1** |
| **½ tsp** | pure vanilla extract | **½ tsp** |
| **20 cl** | plain low-fat yogurt | **7 fl oz** |
| **2 tbsp** | toasted and chopped shelled hazelnuts | **2 tbsp** |
| **1** | lime, rind only, julienned and blanched | **1** |

| | | |
|---|---|---|
| | **Hazelnut Muesli Base** | |
| **3 tbsp** | clear honey | **3 tbsp** |
| **30 g** | unsalted butter | **1 oz** |
| **90 g** | rolled oats | **3 oz** |
| **30 g** | raisins | **1 oz** |
| **1 tbsp** | toasted and chopped shelled hazelnuts | **1 tbsp** |
| **1 tbsp** | chopped dried apples | **1 tbsp** |

Preheat the oven to 170°C (325°F or Mark 3). Grease a 35 by 11 cm (14 by 4½ inch) loose-based plain or fluted oblong tart tin.

To make the muesli base, heat the honey and butter in a saucepan, stirring occasionally. When the butter has melted, remove the pan from the heat and stir in the oats, raisins, hazelnuts and dried apples. Spread the muesli mixture over the base of the tin and level the top with a small palette knife.

Put the soft cheese, honey, egg and vanilla extract in a mixing bowl with all but 3 tablespoons of the yogurt. Mix the ingredients together with a wooden spoon, then beat them until smooth.

Spoon the mixture over the muesli base and level the top with a small palette knife. Bake the cheesecake in the centre of the oven until the filling feels firm when touched in the centre – 20 to 25 minutes.

Remove the cake from the oven and spread the remaining yogurt over the top. Return the cake to the oven for 5 minutes, until the topping has set.

Let the cake cool in the tin. When it reaches room temperature, transfer it to a plate, sprinkle hazelnuts along both sides of the cake and strew the lime julienne down the middle.

# Yule Log

Serves 12

Working
time: about
1 hour

Total time:
about
2 hours and
30 minutes

Calories
175
Protein
2g
Cholesterol
5mg
Total fat
4g
Saturated fat
2g
Sodium
25mg

| 6 | egg whites | 6 |
| 190 g | caster sugar | 6½ oz |
| 90 g | plain chocolate, melted, cooled | 3 oz |
| 60 g | plain flour, sifted | 2 oz |
| | cocoa powder to decorate | |

| | icing sugar to decorate | |
| | **Chestnut Filling** | |
| 200 g | chestnut purée | 7 oz |
| 4 tbsp | single cream | 4 tbsp |
| 1 tbsp | thick honey | 1 tbsp |

Preheat the oven to 220°C (425°F or Mark 7). Place a small piece of non-stick parchment paper on a baking sheet. Grease a 32 by 22 cm (13 by 9 inch) Swiss roll tin and line it with parchment paper. Have ready two piping bags fitted with 1.5 cm (½ inch) plain nozzles.

Whisk egg whites in a bowl to stiff peaks, whisk in 175 g (6 oz) of caster sugar, 1 tablespoon at a time. To make meringue for mushrooms adorning the log, transfer about 3 tablespoons of the mixture into a smaller bowl, and whisk in the remaining sugar. Spoon the smaller quantity of meringue into a piping bag and pipe mushroom stalks and cap on to the parchment paper. Put the baking sheet on the bottom shelf of the oven.

Fold the melted chocolate and the flour into the remaining mixture with a metal spoon. Transfer this mixture to the second piping bag and pipe lines crosswise in the prepared tin. Bake for about 12 minutes, until risen and just firm to the touch. Take it out and switch the oven off, but leave the meringue mushrooms to cool slowly in the oven.

Turn roulade out on a sheet of parchment paper, peel off the lining paper. Loosely replace the lining paper over the cake, cover the cake with the tin and leave to cool completely.

Beat together the chestnut purée, cream and honey until smooth. Detach the cooled mushrooms from the paper and, using some chestnut filling, attach each stalk to a cap.

Remove the tin and lining paper from the cake and spread it with filling. Roll up the log carefully, starting at one short end; use paper to help. Put the log on a dish with mushrooms on and around it. Dust with cocoa and then icing sugar.

# Christmas Garland

| | | |
|---|---|---|
| Serves 16 | | Calories 270 |
| Working time: about 45 minutes | | Protein 6g |
| | | Cholesterol 50mg |
| Total time: about 4 hours | | Total fat 11g |
| | | Saturated fat 2g |
| | | Sodium 65mg |

| | | | | | |
|---|---|---|---|---|---|
| 1 | orange, finely grated rind and juice | 1 | ¼ tsp | ground cinnamon | ¼ tsp |
| 125 g | glacé cherries, chopped | 4 oz | ¼ tsp | ground allspice | ¼ tsp |
| 60 g | mixed candied peel, chopped | 2 oz | ¼ tsp | ground cloves | ¼ tsp |
| 30 g | angelica, chopped | 1 oz | ¼ tsp | grated nutmeg | ¼ tsp |
| 30 g | crystallized pineapple, chopped | 1 oz | 1 tsp | baking powder | 1 tsp |
| 125 g | dried pears, chopped | 4 oz | 3 | eggs, beaten | 3 |
| 60 g | dried apricots, chopped | 2 oz | 1 tbsp | black treacle | 1 tbsp |
| 60 g | sultanas | 2 oz | | | |
| 60 g | currants | 2 oz | | **Icing and Decoration** | |
| 60 g | raisins | 2 oz | 125 g | icing sugar | 4 oz |
| 90 g | shelled walnuts, chopped | 3 oz | 1 tbsp | brandy | 1 tbsp |
| 90 g | shelled Brazil nuts, chopped | 3 oz | 8 | walnut halves | 8 |
| 60 g | shelled almonds, chopped | 2 oz | 4 | glacé cherries, quartered | 4 |
| 125 g | wholemeal flour | 4 oz | | holly leaves for garnish | |

Preheat oven to 150°C (300°F or Mark 2). Grease a 20 cm (8 inch) ring mould.

Put the orange rind and juice in a large bowl. Stir in all the fruit and nuts, the mixed peel and angelica. Sift the flour, cinnamon, allspice, cloves, nutmeg and baking powder, adding the bran left in the sieve. Pour in eggs and treacle and beat well. Transfer the mixture to the prepared mould and press it down.

Bake cake for 45 minutes, or until firm to touch. Leave in the tin for 10 minutes, invert it on to a wire tray and leave to cool completely.

To make the icing, mix the icing sugar with the brandy and a little water, if necessary, to give a thin coating consistency. Spoon the icing over the cake, then decorate the cake with the walnut halves, cherry quarters and holly leaves.

# Hazelnut and Raspberry Galette

**Serves 12**

**Working time: about 1 hour**

**Total time: about 2 hours**

**Calories 165**

**Protein 5g**

**Cholesterol 65mg**

**Total fat 8g**

**Saturated fat 3g**

**Sodium 70mg**

| | | |
|---|---|---|
| **3** | eggs | **3** |
| **30 g** | caster sugar | **1 oz** |
| **30 g** | wholemeal flour | **1 oz** |
| **½ tsp** | pure vanilla extract | **½ tsp** |
| **250 g** | thick Greek yogurt | **8 oz** |
| **300 g** | fresh raspberries, or frozen raspberries, thawed | **10 oz** |
| **4 tbsp** | double cream, whipped | **4 tbsp** |

| | **Hazelnut Meringue** | |
|---|---|---|
| **3** | egg whites | **3** |
| **⅛ tsp** | salt | **⅛ tsp** |
| **90 g** | caster sugar | **3 oz** |
| **90 g** | shelled hazelnuts, toasted, skinned and finely chopped | **3 oz** |
| **1 tbsp** | cornflour | **1 tbsp** |

Preheat oven to 200°C (400°F or Mark 6). Grease two 32 by 22 cm (13 by 9 inch) Swiss roll tins. Line them with lightly-greased non-stick parchment paper.

Whisk egg whites with salt until mixture stands in stiff peaks, then gradually whisk in sugar 1 tablespoon at a time, whisking between each addition. Mix hazelnuts with cornflour and fold into meringue. Spread meringue evenly in one of the prepared tins and bake it for 20 minutes. Leave it to cool in the tin. Reduce the oven to 180°C (350°F or Mark 4).

Whisk the eggs and sugar in a bowl over a pan of simmering water until pale and thick. Remove from the heat and whisk until cool. Fold in the flour and vanilla, transfer to second tin and level surface. Bake the sponge for about 15 minutes, until just firm to the touch. Leave it to cool.

Remove sponge and meringue from their tins. Trim them to the same size. Cut each in half lengthwise. Crumble meringue trimmings and stir them into the yogurt. Spread the yogurt over one layer of meringue and both layers of sponge.

Reserve 30 raspberries, divide the remainder among the three layers spread with yogurt. Place a sponge layer on a dish, cover with decorated meringue layer, then the second sponge layer and finally the remaining meringue layer. Press down gently. Using a piping bag with a medium star nozzle, pipe lines of cream across the top. Arrange the raspberries between the cream.

# Meringue Coffee Torte

Serves 12

Working
time: about
50 minutes

Total time:
about
2 hours and
30 minutes

Calories
165

Protein
10g

Cholesterol
45mg

Total fat
6g

Saturated fat
1g

Sodium
220mg

| | | |
|---|---|---|
| 30 g | light brown sugar | 1 oz |
| 2 | eggs | 2 |
| 60 g | brown flour | 2 oz |
| ½ tsp | baking powder | ½ tsp |
| 300 g | skimmed-milk soft cheese | 10 oz |
| 4 tbsp | double cream | 4 tbsp |
| 1 tbsp | clear honey | 1 tbsp |
| 3 tsp | strong black coffee | 3 tsp |

| | | |
|---|---|---|
| | icing sugar to decorate | |
| 18 | walnut halves | 18 |
| | | |
| | **Walnut Meringue** | |
| 2 | egg whites | 2 |
| 90 g | demerara sugar | 3 oz |
| 45 g | shelled walnuts, finely chopped | 1½ oz |
| 2 tsp | cornflour | 2 tsp |

Preheat oven to 180°C (350°F or Mark 4). Grease a 20 cm (8 inch) round cake tin. Line its base with greased greaseproof paper.

Put brown sugar and eggs in a bowl set over simmering water. Whisk mixture until thick and pale. Remove bowl from heat and whisk until whisk, when lifted, leaves a trail. Sift flour and baking powder into mixture. Pour mixture into prepared tin and level.

Bake sponge in centre of oven until risen, lightly coloured and springy to touch – 15 to 20 minutes. Leave for 5 minutes, then turn cake out on to a wire rack. Remove paper and leave to cool.

Reduce oven setting to 130°C (250°F or Mark ½). Line a baking sheet with non-stick parchment paper. Draw two 18.5 cm (7½ inch) circles on the parchment

and invert it. In a bowl, whisk the egg whites until they hold stiff peaks. Add ⅓ of the sugar at a time, whisking well after each addition. Mix together the walnuts and cornflour, and fold into the meringue.

Divide the walnut meringue between the two circles and spread it evenly. Bake the rounds for 1 hour to 1 hour and 20 minutes, until the meringue feels firm and dry. Cool on a wire rack, then remove parchment.

Beat together cheese and cream; add honey and coffee. Put 2 tbsps coffee cream into piping bag.

Split sponge into two halves, and arrange alternate layers of meringue, coffee cream and sponge on a plate, ending with sponge.

Dust top with icing sugar and decorate with piped coffee cream and walnut halves.

# Date and Apricot Triangles

Serves 24

Working time: about 40 minutes

Total time: about 2 hours and 40 minutes

Calories 200

Protein 3g

Cholesterol 30mg

Total fat 8g

Saturated fat 2g

Sodium 60mg

| | | |
|---|---|---|
| 250 g | dried apricots, chopped | 8 oz |
| 250 g | dried dates, chopped | 8 oz |
| 125 g | raisins | 4 oz |
| 3 tbsp | malt extract | 3 tbsp |
| 125 g | polyunsaturated margarine | 4 oz |
| 125 g | dark brown sugar | 4 oz |
| 3 | large eggs | 3 |
| 200 g | wholemeal flour | 7 oz |
| 1 tsp | ground cinnamon | 1 tsp |
| ½ tsp | ground nutmeg | ½ tsp |
| 1 tbsp | apricot jam without added sugar | 1 tbsp |
| **Hazelnut Paste** | | |
| 150 g | hazelnuts, skinned and ground | 5 oz |
| 150 g | caster sugar | 5 oz |
| 60 g | ground rice | 2 oz |
| 1 | large egg white | 1 |
| 2 tsp | rose water | 2 tsp |

Preheat oven to 170°C (325°F or Mark 3). Grease a 28 by 18 cm (11 by 7 inch) baking tin. Line it with greaseproof paper and grease paper. Cover the apricots with boiling water, leave to soak for 30 minutes. Drain.

Put fruit in a bowl, stir in malt. In another bowl, beat the margarine and brown sugar until fluffy, beat in eggs one at a time, adding a little flour with each egg. Mix in remaining flour, cinnamon, nutmeg and fruits.

Turn batter into baking tin and smooth to edges. Bake cake for 30 minutes, reduce the heat to 150°C (300°F or Mark 2) and cook for a further 40 minutes until firm in centre. Turn on to a wire rack to cool. Remove paper.

Mix the hazelnuts, caster sugar and ground rice together. Make a well in the centre and stir in the egg white and rose water until the mixture binds together.

Heat jam with ½ tablespoon of water and sieve. Brush over base of cake while glaze is still warm. Roll hazelnut paste out to a rectangle same size as cake, using ground rice to prevent it from sticking to board. Drape paste rectangle over rolling pin and transfer to cake. Neaten edges, make a lattice pattern on top of paste. Put cake under a hot grill for 1 to 2 minutes, until the paste is tinged brown. Cut into triangles to serve.

# Honey Squares

Serves 24

Working time: about 30 minutes

Total time: about 1 hour and 40 minutes

Calories 160
Protein 3g
Cholesterol 5mg
Total fat 8g
Saturated fat 1g
Sodium 85mg

| | | |
|---|---|---:|
| 250 g | plain flour | 8 oz |
| 3 tsp | baking powder | 3 tsp |
| 125 g | wholemeal flour | 4 oz |
| 2 | lemons, finely grated rind only | 2 |
| 190 g | clear honey | 6½ oz |
| 60 g | unsalted butter | 2 oz |
| 6 tbsp | safflower oil | 6 tbsp |
| 60 g | dark muscovado sugar | 2 oz |

| | | |
|---|---|---:|
| 1 | egg | 1 |
| 1 | egg white | 1 |
| 6 tbsp | buttermilk | 6 tbsp |
| 6 tbsp | skimed milk | 6 tbsp |
| 30 g | blanched almonds, split and lightly toasted | 1 oz |
| 6 | glacé cherries, quartered | 6 |
| 15 g | angelica, cut into leaf shapes | ½ oz |

Preheat the oven to 180°C (350°F or Mark 4). Grease a rectangular 30 by 20 by 3 cm (12 by 8 by 1¼ inch) baking tin and line it with non-stick parchment paper.

Sift the plain flour and baking powder into a bowl; mix in the wholemeal flour and lemon rind and make a well in the centre.

Reserving 1 tablespoon of honey, put the remainder into a saucepan with the butter, oil and sugar. Heat gently until the butter is melted. Let the mixture cool slightly. Very lightly whisk the egg and the egg white together, then whisk in the buttermilk and milk. Pour the honey and egg mixtures into the centre of the flour. Stir well, then pour the batter into the prepared tin, spreading it evenly.

Bake the honey cake for 35 to 40 minutes, until well risen, firm and springy to the touch. Remove it from the oven and immediately brush the top with the reserved tablespoonful of honey. Arrange the almonds, glacé cherries and angelica leaves on the cake. Cut the cake into squares when it has cooled.

# Fig Bars

Serves 18

Working time: about 25 minutes

Total time: about 2 hours

Calories 145
Protein 3g
Cholesterol 0mg
Total fat 9g
Saturated fat 2g
Sodium 85mg

| | | | |
|---|---|---|---|
| 300 g | dried figs, finely chopped | 10 oz | |
| 5 tbsp | apple juice | 5 tbsp | |
| 150 g | wholemeal flour | 5 oz | |
| 150 g | polyunsaturated margarine | 5 oz | |

| | | | |
|---|---|---|---|
| 150 g | rolled oats | 5 oz | |
| 45 g | muscovado sugar | 1½ oz | |
| 2 tbsp | sesame seeds, browned | 2 tbsp | |

Preheat the oven to 190°C (375°F or Mark 5). Grease and line a 20 cm (8 inch) square shallow baking tin.

Put the figs in a saucepan with the apple juice and simmer for 5 minutes, stirring occasionally, until the figs are soft. Set the pan aside. Put the flour and margarine in a bowl and blend them together with a fork. Add the oats, sugar and sesame seeds and rub the mixture until it resembles coarse breadcrumbs.

Press half of the oat mixture into the tin. Spread the figs and apple juice on top, then sprinkle over the remaining oat mixture. Press the top oat layer down firmly with a palette knife. Bake the fig cake for 40 to 50 minutes, until its top is golden.

Cut the cake into bars while warm, but leave them in the tin to cool completely.

*Suggested Accompaniment:* chilled apple juice.

*Editor's Note:* To brown sesame seeds, sprinkle a layer of seeds in a heavy-based pan, cover and cook over high heat. When they begin to pop, keep the pan on the heat for 1 minute more but shake it constantly.

# Coconut Bars

Serves 20

Working time: about 25 minutes

Total time: about 1 hour and 45 minutes

Calories 100

Protein 2g

Cholesterol 36mg

Total fat 4g

Saturated fat 3g

Sodium 18mg

| 3 | eggs, separated | 3 |
|---|---|---|
| 125 g | caster sugar | 4 oz |
| ½ | lemon, grated rind and juice | ½ |
| 60 g | semolina | 2 oz |
| 30 g | ground almonds | 1 oz |

| | **Chewy Coconut Topping** | |
|---|---|---|
| 2 | egg whites | 2 |
| 90 g | demerara sugar | 3 oz |
| 90 g | desiccated coconut | 3 oz |

Preheat the oven to 180°C (350°F or Mark 4). Grease a 28 by 18 cm (11 by 7 inch) baking tin, line its base with greaseproof paper and grease the paper.

Cream the egg yolks with the sugar, lemon rind and juice the mixture is thick. Stir in the semolina and ground almonds. Whisk the egg whites until they are stiff, then fold them into the creamed mixture. Turn the batter into the baking tin and level the batter's surface.

To make the topping, whisk the two egg whites until they are stiff, then fold in the demerara sugar and coconut. Lay dessertspoons of the topping at regular intervals on top of the cake batter. (Larger spoonfuls would sink down into the light sponge mixture.) With a fork, carefully tease the topping into an even layer that reaches to the tin's edge.

Bake the coconut cake for 35 to 40 minutes, until golden. Turn the cake out on to a rack; the coconut topping will be quite firm, and will not crumble. Remove the lining paper, then reverse the cake again on to a second rack. When the cake is cool, cut it into bars with a sharp, serrated knife.

# Apple Streusel Slices

Serves 20

Working
time: about
40 minutes

Total time:
about
2 hours

Calories
135

Protein
2g

Cholesterol
0mg

Total fat
5g

Saturated fat
1g

Sodium
55mg

| | | |
|---|---|---|
| 100 g | polyunsaturated margarine | 3½ oz |
| 200 g | wholemeal flour | 7 oz |
| 750 g | dessert apples, peeled, cored and chopped | 1½ lb |
| 60 g | dark brown sugar | 2 oz |
| 2 tsp | ground cinnamon | 2 tsp |
| 90 g | sultanas | 3 oz |

| | Sesame Streusel | |
|---|---|---|
| 30 g | polyunsaturated margarine | 1 oz |
| 75 g | wholemeal flour | 2½ oz |
| 30 g | demerara sugar | 1 oz |
| 1½ tbsp | sesame seeds | 1½ tbsp |
| 1 tsp | ground cinnamon | 2 tsp |

Rub the margarine into the flour in a bowl until the mixture resembles breadcrumbs. Stir in about 3 tablespoons of iced water – enough to make a fairly firm dough – and knead lightly until the dough is smooth. Wrap the dough in plastic film and leave it to rest for 10 minutes.

Roll the dough out thinly on a lightly floured surface, and use it to line a 30 by 20 cm (12 by 8 inch) Swiss roll tin. Prick the dough with a fork and refrigerate it for about 15 minutes.

Meanwhile, preheat the oven to 200°C (400°F or Mark 6). Put the chopped apples in a bowl, with the sugar, cinnamon and sultanas, and mix them together.

To make the sesame streusel, rub the margarine into the flour in a bowl until the mixture resembles breadcrumbs. Stir in the sugar, sesame seeds and cinnamon. Sprinkle 3 tablespoons of the mixture over the dough in the tin to absorb the juice from the apples. Spread the apple mixture in the tin. Sprinkle the remaining streusel over the apples. Bake the cake for 30 to 35 minutes, until the streusel is golden-brown. Cut the cake into slices when it has cooled.

# Almond-Apricot Fingers

**Serves 18**

Working
time: about
30 minutes

Total time:
about
2 hours

Calories
150

Protein
3g

Cholesterol
25mg

Total fat
9g

Saturated fat
2g

Sodium
100mg

| | | |
|---|---|---|
| **125 g** | wholemeal flour | **4 oz** |
| **2 tsp** | baking powder | **2 tsp** |
| **125 g** | polyunsaturated margarine | **4 oz** |
| **175 g** | dried apricots, chopped and soaked for 30 minutes in boiling water | **6 oz** |
| **90 g** | light muscovado sugar | **3 oz** |
| **2** | eggs | **2** |
| **60 g** | ground almonds | **2 oz** |
| **½ tsp** | almond extract | **½ tsp** |
| **30 g** | flaked almonds | **1 oz** |

Preheat the oven to 190°C (375°F or Mark 5) Line the base of a 30 by 20 cm (12 by 8 inch) baking tin with greaseproof paper and grease the paper.

Sift the wholemeal flour with the baking powder, adding the bran left in the sieve. Cream the margarine and sugar together in a bowl until fluffy. Beat in the eggs one at a time, adding 1 tablespoon of the flour mixture with each egg.

Drain the apricots thoroughly, reserving 1 tablespoon of the soaking liquid. Stir the apricots into the batter and fold in the remaining flour mixture, together with the ground almonds, almond extract and reserved apricot soaking liquid. Turn the mixture into the baking tin. Spread it evenly to the edges and sprinkle the flaked almonds over the top.

Bake the cake for 30 to 35 minutes, until it springs back when pressed in the centre. Turn the cake out on to a wire rack, remove the lining paper, then reverse the cake on to another rack to cool. Cut the cake into fingers when it has cooled.

# Apricot Tray Bake

**Serves 16**

**Working time: about 45 minutes**

**Total time: about 3 hours**

Calories
200

Protein
7g

Cholesterol
25mg

Total fat
11g

Saturated fat
4g

Sodium
75mg

| | | |
|---|---|---|
| **250 g** | medium-fat curd cheese | **8 oz** |
| **45 g** | caster sugar | **1½ oz** |
| **1** | egg, beaten | **1** |
| **125 g** | ground almonds | **4 oz** |
| **1** | lemon, finely grated rind only | **1** |
| **16** | large apricots | **16** |
| **15 g** | icing sugar | **½ oz** |
| **15 g** | pistachio nuts, skinned and very finely sliced | **½ oz** |

| | | |
|---|---|---|
| **1 tbsp** | apricot jam without added sugar | **1 tbsp** |
| | **Yeast dough** | |
| **175 g** | plain flour | **6 oz** |
| **30 g** | vanilla sugar | **1 oz** |
| **1** | lemon, finely grated rind only | **1** |
| **60 g** | unsalted butter | **2 oz** |
| **15 g** | fresh yeast or 7 g (¼ oz) dried yeast | **½ oz** |
| **6 tbsp** | skimmed milk, tepid | **6 tbsp** |

Sift flour into a bowl, mix in vanilla-flavoured sugar and lemon rind, rub in butter until mixture resembles fine breadcrumbs. Dissolve yeast in tepid milk; if using dried yeast, follow manufacturer's instructions. Pour yeast liquid into flour and mix to form a soft dough. On a floured surface, knead dough for 2 to 3 minutes to smooth. Put dough in a clean bowl. Cover with film and leave in a warm place for 1 hour until doubled in size.

Knead risen dough for 1 minute, roll it out to form an oblong large enough to fit a 32 by 22 by 2 cm (13 by 9 by ¾ inch) baking tray. Butter the tray. Press dough into tray to fit exactly and prick all over with a fork. Cover with film and leave in a warm place for 30 to 40 minutes, until the dough has risen slightly.

Heat the oven to 200°C (400°F or Mark 6). Beat curd cheese in a bowl with caster sugar, egg, almonds and lemon rind until smooth. Spread evenly over dough.

Simmer apricots for 10 to 15 secs to loosen skins. Remove apricots, skin, halve and stone. Arrange, evenly, on top of cheese mixture. Sift icing sugar over apricots. Leave for 2 mins to dissolve sugar; bake cake for 30 to 35 mins, until set and lightly browned and the apricots are soft.

Brush boiling apricot jam over apricots and sprinkle with pistachios. Allow to cool completely in tin, then slice.

# Coffee Butterfly Cakes

**Makes 12 cakes**

**Working time: about 35 minutes**

**Total time: about 1 hour and 30 minutes**

*Per cake:*

Calories
180

Protein
2g

Cholesterol
20mg

Total fat
9g

Saturated fat
5g

Sodium
45mg

| | | |
|---|---|---|
| **125 g** | unsalted butter | **4 oz** |
| **60 g** | light brown sugar | **2 oz** |
| **60 g** | clear honey | **2 oz** |
| **2 tbsp** | strong black coffee | **2 tbsp** |
| **2** | egg whites, lightly beaten | **2** |

| | | |
|---|---|---|
| **175 g** | plain flour | **6 oz** |
| **1½ tsp** | baking powder | **1½ tsp** |
| **15 cl** | rum-flavoured pastry cream (see page 7) | **¼ pint** |
| **1 tsp** | icing sugar | **1 tsp** |

Preheat the oven to 180°C (350°F or Mark 4). Butter 12 deep, sloping-sided bun tins. Dust the tins lightly with a little flour.

Cream the butter in a bowl with the brown sugar and honey until soft. Add the black coffee and 1 tablespoon of warm water, and continue beating until the mixture becomes very light and fluffy. Gradually beat in the egg whites. Sift the flour and baking powder together over the creamed mixture, then fold them in carefully with a metal spoon or rubber spatula.

Divide the mixture evenly among the prepared tins. Bake the cakes for 15 to 20 minutes, until well risen, springy to the touch and very slightly

shrunk from the sides of the tins. Leave the cakes in the tins for 2 to 3 minutes, then transfer them to a wire rack to cool.

Using a small, sharp pointed knife held at an angle, carefully cut a cone out of the centre of each cake. Cut each cone in half.

Put the rum-flavoured pastry cream in a piping bag fitted with a medium-sized star nozzle. Pipe a whirl of pastry cream into the middle of each cake. Then replace the two halves of each cone on top of the cream, angling them to mimic butterfly wings. Sift the icing sugar lightly over the cakes.

# Cherry and Walnut Buns

Makes 24
buns

Working
time: about
25 minutes

Total time:
about
2 hours and
45 minutes

Per bun:

Calories
140

Protein
3g

Cholesterol
20mg

Total fat
6g

Saturated fat
3g

Sodium
15mg

| | | |
|---|---|---|
| **60 g** | glacé cherries, chopped | **2 oz** |
| **125 g** | dried dates, stoned and chopped | **4 oz** |
| **2 tbsp** | rum | **2 tbsp** |
| **250 g** | plain flour | **8 oz** |
| **⅛ tsp** | salt | **⅛ tsp** |
| **125 g** | wholemeal flour | **4 oz** |
| **60 g** | light brown sugar | **2 oz** |
| **60 g** | unsalted butter | **2 oz** |

| | | |
|---|---|---|
| **1** | lemon, finely grated rind only | **1** |
| **15 g** | fresh yeast or 7 g (¼ oz) dried yeast | **½ oz** |
| **¼ litre** | skimmed milk, tepid | **8 fl oz** |
| **1** | egg | **1** |
| **4 tbsp** | safflower oil | **4 tbsp** |
| **60 g** | shelled walnuts, chopped | **2 oz** |
| **1 tsp** | icing sugar | **1 tsp** |

Put cherries and dates into a small bowl with the rum and mix well. Cover the fruit and set it aside.

Sift plain flour and salt into a bowl. Mix in the wholemeal flour and brown sugar. Rub butter into flours until mixture resembles fine breadcrumbs. Mix in lemon rind. Dissolve yeast in the milk; if using dried yeast, leave to stand, following, manufacturer's instructions. Whisk egg and oil together. Pour yeast liquid and egg mixture into flours and beat dough with a wooden spoon or electric beater until smooth and elasticated – about 5 minutes. Cover with plastic film and leave dough in a warm place for 1 hour until doubled in size. Meanwhile, butter and lightly flour two 12-hole deep bun tin trays.

Beat the dates and cherries, and 30 g (1 oz) of the walnuts into the risen dough. Divide the dough evenly among the prepared bun tins. Cover loosely with plastic film and leave in a warm place until the dough rises to the top of the tins – 30 to 40 minutes. Meanwhile, preheat the oven to 200°C (400°F or Mark 6).

When the dough has risen to the top of the tins, sprinkle the remaining walnuts on top of the buns and bake them for 20 to 25 minutes, until well risen, golden-brown and slightly shrunk from the sides of the tins. Turn the buns on to wire racks. When they have cooled, sift the icing sugar over the buns.

# Banana and Cardamom Cakes

**Makes 18 cakes**

**Working time: about 20 minutes**

**Total time: about 50 minutes**

*Per cake:*

Calories
145

Protein
3g

Cholesterol
25mg

Total fat
9g

Saturated fat
2g

Sodium
115mg

| | | |
|---|---|---|
| **125 g** | polyunsaturated margarine | **4 oz** |
| **90 g** | brown sugar | **3 oz** |
| **10** | cardamom pods, seeds only, finely chopped | **10** |
| **125 g** | wholemeal flour | **4 oz** |
| **2 tsp** | baking powder | **2 tsp** |
| **2** | eggs | **2** |
| **2** | medium bananas, mashed | **2** |
| **60 g** | ground almonds | **2 oz** |

### Creamy Topping

| | | |
|---|---|---|
| **90 g** | medium-fat curd cheese | **3 oz** |
| **2 tsp** | clear honey | **2 tsp** |
| **1 tbsp** | plain low-fat yogurt | **1 tbsp** |

Preheat the oven to 190°C (375°F or Mark 5). Grease and flour 18 bun tins.

In a bowl, cream the margarine and sugar together with the cardamom seeds until the mixture is fluffy. Sift the flour with the baking powder, adding the bran left in the sieve. With a wooden spoon, beat the eggs into the margarine and sugar one at a time, adding a tablespoon of the flour with each egg. Beat in the bananas and almonds, then fold in the remaining flour.

Divide the batter among the bun tins and bake the cake for 15 minutes, until the centre springs back when pressed. Loosen the cakes from the tins with a small knife and put them on a wire rack to cool.

To make the topping, beat the curd cheese with the honey and yogurt. When the blend is smooth, spoon it into a piping bag fitted with a medium-sized star nozzle and pipe a rosette on each cake.

# Cinnamon Rock Cakes

Makes 16 cakes

Working time: about 20 minutes

Total time: about 1 hour

Per cake:

Calories 135

Protein 3g

Cholesterol 25mg

Total fat 4g

Saturated fat 2g

Sodium 90mg

| | | | | | | |
|---|---|---|---|---|---|---|
| 125 g | plain flour | 4 oz | | 60 g | unsalted butter | 2 oz |
| 2 tsp | baking powder | 2 tsp | | 90 g | raisins | 3 oz |
| ½ tsp | grated nutmeg | ½ tsp | | 90 g | sultanas | 3 oz |
| 1 tsp | ground cinnamon | 1 tsp | | 1 | egg, beaten | 1 |
| 125 g | wholemeal flour | 4 oz | | 2 tbsp | plain low-fat yogurt | 2 tbsp |
| 60 g | dark brown sugar | 2 oz | | 6 tbsp | skimmed milk | 6tbsp |
| 1 | lemon, finely grated rind only | 1 | | 2 tsp | caster sugar | 2 tsp |

Preheat the oven to 220°C (425°F or Mark 7). Butter and lightly flour two baking sheets.

Sift the plain flour, baking powder, nutmeg and half of the cinnamon into a bowl. Mix in the wholemeal flour, brown sugar and lemon rind. Rub the butter into the flours until the mixture resembles fine breadcrumbs. Mix in the raisins and sultanas, then make a well into the centre. Put the egg, yogurt and milk into the well and stir to form a fairly soft mixture.

Space heaped teaspoons of the mixture well apart on the prepared baking sheets. Bake for 15 to 20 minutes until the rock cakes are well risen, golden-brown and firm to the touch. Transfer the rock cakes from the baking trays to wire racks to cool.

Mix the caster sugar with the remaining cinnamon and sprinkle the combination over the rock cakes.

# Spiced Teacakes

**Makes 12 teacakes**

**Working time: about 50 minutes**

**Total time: about 2 hours and 40 minutes**

*Per teacake:*

Calories
235

Protein
6g

Cholesterol
30mg

Total fat
5g

Saturated fat
3g

Sodium
30mg

| | | | | | | |
|---|---|---:|---|---|---:|
| 250 g | plain flour | 8 oz | 60 g | light brown sugar | 2 oz |
| ½ tsp | salt | ½ tsp | 30 g | unsalted butter | 1 oz |
| ½ tsp | grated nutmeg | ½ tsp | 30 g | fresh yeast, or 15 g (½ oz) dried | 1 oz |
| ¼ tsp | ground cloves | ¼ tsp | 1 | egg, beaten | 1 |
| ½ tsp | ground cinnamon | ½ tsp | 6 tbsp | soured cream | 6 tbsp |
| ½ tsp | ground allspice | ½ tsp | 60 g | currants | 2 oz |
| ¼ tsp | ground mace | ¼ tsp | 60 g | sultanas | 2 oz |
| 250 g | wholemeal flour | 8 oz | 2 tbsp | clear honey | 2 tbsp |

Sift the plain flour, salt and spices into a large bowl. Mix in the wholemeal flour and sugar. Rub the butter into the flours and make a well in the centre of the mixture. Dissolve the yeast in 15 cl (¼ pint) of tepid water; if using dried yeast, follow manufacturer's instructions. Pour the yeast liquid into the centre of the flour and add the egg and soured cream. Mix to form a soft dough.

Knead the dough on a lightly floured surface for about 10 minutes, until smooth and elastic. Put the dough in a clean bowl. Cover with plastic film and leave in a warm place for about 1 hour, until dough has doubled in size. Meanwhile, butter and lightly flour three baking sheets.

Knock back the risen dough, then knead in the fruit. Divide dough into 12 pieces. Knead and shape each piece into a smooth ball. Roll with a rolling pin into flat rounds about 10 cm (4 inches) in diameter and place four on each baking sheet. Prick the rounds well with a fork.

Loosely cover the teacakes with plastic film and leave them in a warm place for about 30 minutes, until doubled in size. Meanwhile, preheat the oven to 220°C (425°F or Mark 7).

Bake the teacakes for 15 to 20 minutes, until they are golden-brown and sound hollow when lightly tapped on the base. Remove from the oven and brush with honey. Cool on wire racks.

# Rum Babas

**Makes 12
babas**

**Working
time: about
50 minutes**

**Total time:
about
4 hours**

*Per baba:*
**Calories
175
Protein
4g
Cholesterol
30mg
Total fat
4g
Saturated fat
2g
Sodium
90mg**

| | | |
|---|---|---|
| **175 g** | plain flour | **6 oz** |
| **¼ tsp** | salt | **¼ tsp** |
| **15 g** | caster sugar | **½ oz** |
| **15 g** | fresh yeast, or 7 g (¼ oz) dried | **½ oz** |
| **5 tbsp** | skimmed milk, tepid | **5 tbsp** |
| **1** | egg | **1** |
| **2** | egg whites | **2** |
| **1** | orange, finely grated rind only | **1** |
| **45 g** | unsalted butter, softened | **1½ oz** |

| | | |
|---|---|---|
| **4 tbsp** | thick Greek yogurt, chilled | **4 tbsp** |
| **3** | oranges, rind and pith removed, flesh cut into segments | **3** |
| | **Syrup** | |
| **1** | orange, strained juice only | **1** |
| **90 g** | light brown sugar | **3 oz** |
| **125 g** | clear honey | **4 oz** |
| **4 tbsp** | rum | **4 tbsp** |

Dissolve yeast in milk and sugar. (For dried yeast, follow manufacturer's instructions.) Stand mixture in a warm place until bubbles appear – 30 minutes. Sift flour and salt into a bowl; make a well in the centre. Pour in yeast liquid, lightly beaten eggs and whites, melted butter and orange rind and beat thoroughly (about 5 mins) to a smooth, elastic dough.

Grease, flour and warm twelve fluted moulds (7.5 by 3 cm or 3 by 1¼ inches) and divide the dough between them. Leave in a warm place for 30 – 40 minutes until dough reaches top of moulds.

Bake in a hot oven 200°C (400°F or Mark 6) for 15 to 20 minutes until babas are golden brown, firm to touch and slightly shrunken. Cool in moulds for a few minutes, then turn out and cool on a wire rack.

While babas are cooking, heat orange juice, brown sugar and honey with 45 cl (¾ pint) water until sugar is dissolved, stirring occasionaly. Boil for 5 minutes until thick. Stir in rum. Cut cones from the top of the babas, and drench them with syrup. Spoon yogurt into centres, decorate with orange segments and replace tops.

# Fairy Cakes

Makes 12
cakes

Working
time: about
30 minutes

Total time:
about
1 hour and
15 minutes

Per plain,
cherry or
sultana
(coconut)
cake:

Calories
195 (205)

Protein
2g (3g)

Cholesterol
25mg

Total fat
8g (12g)

Saturated fat
2g (5g)

Sodium
160mg
(155mg)

| 125 g | polyunsaturated margarine | 4 oz | 15 g | glacé cherries, chopped | ½ oz |
| 60 g | caster sugar | 2 oz | 15 g | desiccated coconut | ½ oz |
| 60 g | clear honey | 2 oz | 30 g | sultanas | 1 oz |
| 1 tsp | pure vanilla extract | 1 tsp | 15 cl | pastry cream | ¼ pint |
| 2 | egg whites, lightly beaten | 2 | 1 | hazelnut, thinly sliced | 1 |
| 175 g | plain flour | 6 oz | | chocolate curls for garnish | |
| 1½ tsp | baking powder | 1½ tsp | | | |

Preheat the oven to 190°C (375°F or Mark 5). Grease and lightly flour 12 deep, sloping-sided bun tins.

Put the margarine, sugar and honey in a bowl. With a wooden spoon, beat them until they are soft and creamy. Beat in the vanilla extract with 3 tablespoons of warm water; continue beating until the mixture becomes very light and fluffy. Gradually beat in the egg whites. Sift the flour and baking powder over the creamed mixture, then fold them in carefully with a metal spoon or rubber spatula.

Half fill three of the bun tins with the plain mixture. Divide the remaining mixture equally into three. To one third add the cherries, reserving

three pieces; to another third add the coconut, reserving 2 teaspoons; to the remaining third, add the sultanas. Spoon the mixture into the bun tins. Bake for 10 to 15 minutes until the fairy cakes are well risen, golden-brown and springy to the touch. Leave them in the tins for 2 to 3 minutes, then transfer them to wire racks.

When the cakes have cooled, put the pastry cream into a piping bag fitted with a medium-sized star nozzle. Pipe a shell shape on top of each cake. Decorate the plain cakes with the hazelnut slices, the cherry cakes with the reserved cherry pieces, the coconut cakes with the reserved coconut, and the sultana cakes with the chocolate curls.

# Madeleines

Makes 20
madeleines

Working
time: about
10 minutes

Total time:
about
35 minutes

*Per
madeleine:*

Calories
65

Protein
1g

Cholesterol
30mg

Total fat
2g

Saturated fat
1g

Sodium
10mg

| 1 | egg | 1 | 90 g | plain flour | 3 oz |
|---|---|---|---|---|---|
| 1 | egg white | 1 | 45 g | unsalted butter, melted and cooled | 1½ oz |
| 90 g | caster sugar | 3 oz | 1 tbsp | vanilla sugar | 1 tbsp |
| 1 tbsp | amaretto liqueur | 1 tbsp | | | |

Preheat the oven to 200°C (400°F or Mark 6). Butter twenty 7.5 cm (3 inch) madeleine moulds and dust them lightly with flour.

Put the egg and egg white into a bowl with the caster sugar and amaretto. Whisk the mixture until it thickens to the consistency of unwhipped double cream. Sift the flour lightly over the surface of the mixture, then fold it in very carefully with a metal spoon or rubber spatula.

Gently fold in the melted butter.

Half fill each madeleine mould with mixture. Bake the madeleines for 15 to 20 minutes, until well risen, lightly browned and springy to the touch. Carefully turn them out of the moulds on to a wire rack and immediately sift the vanilla sugar over them. Serve the madeleines while still warm, or allow them to cool.

# Raspberry-Filled Shells

Makes 18
shells

Working
time: about
40 minutes

Total time:
about
1 hour and
40 minutes

Per shell:

Calories
107

Protein
2g

Cholesterol
50mg

Total fat
6g

Saturated fat
3g

Sodium
20mg

| | | |
|---|---|---|
| **3** | eggs | **3** |
| **90 g** | caster sugar | **3 oz** |
| **90 g** | plain flour | **3 oz** |
| **¼ litre** | whipping cream, whipped | **8 fl oz** |

| | | |
|---|---|---|
| **350 g** | fresh raspberries, or frozen raspberries, thawed | **12 oz** |
| **1 tbsp** | icing sugar | **1 tbsp** |

Preheat the oven to 180°C (350°F or Mark 4). Grease 18 rounded, shell-patterned bun moulds and dust the moulds lightly with flour.

To make the sponge, put the eggs and caster sugar in a large bowl. Place the bowl over a saucepan of hot, but not boiling, water on a low heat. Whisk until the mixture becomes thick and very pale in colour. Remove the bowl from the heat and continue whisking until the mixture is cool and will hold a ribbon trail almost indefinitely. Sift flour very lightly over the top of the whisked mixture and fold it in carefully with a large metal spoon or a rubber spatula.

Divide the sponge batter equally among the 18 bun moulds and spread it evenly. Bake the sponges for 25 to 30 minutes until very well risen, lightly browned and springy to the touch. Turn the sponges out of the moulds on to a wire rack to cool, rounded sides up.

Cut each sponge in half, at a slight angle to the horizontal. Cover the bottom halves with cream and raspberries and set the top halves with on the filling at an angle, so that the cakes resemble half open clams. Sift the icing sugar over the cakes.

# Strawberry Galettes

Makes 12
galettes

Working
time: about
1 hour

Total time:
about
2 hours and
10 minutes

*Per galette:*

Calories
185

Protein
6g

Cholesterol
95mg

Total fat
7g

Saturated fat
3g

Sodium
80mg

| | | |
|---|---|---|
| **4** | eggs | **4** |
| **1** | egg white | **1** |
| **150 g** | caster sugar | **5 oz** |
| **150 g** | plain flour | **5 oz** |
| **60 g** | unsalted butter, melted and cooled | **2 oz** |

| | | |
|---|---|---|
| **15 cl** | double cream | **¼ pint** |
| **1 tsp** | pure vanilla extract | **1 tsp** |
| **2 tbsp** | icing sugar | **2 tbsp** |
| **200 g** | fromage frais | **7 oz** |
| **500 g** | strawberries, hulled, all but six sliced | **1 lb** |

Preheat oven to 180°C (350°F or Mark 4). Butter a 38 by 28 by 2 cm (15 by 11 by ¾ inch) baking tin. Line the base with parchment paper.

Put eggs and egg white into a bowl with sugar over a pan of hot, but not boiling, water. Whisk until thick and very pale. Remove bowl from heat and continue whisking until mixture is cool and will hold a trail. Lightly sift flour over surface of mixture, fold in carefully. Gradually fold butter into the mixture.

Pour sponge mixture into tin and level. Bake sponge for 30 to 35 minutes until risen, lightly browned and springy to touch. Turn out of tin on to a cooling rack and loosen paper. Place another rack on top of paper and invert both racks together so that paper is underneath. Remove top rack.

To make filling, put double cream, vanilla extract and 1 tablespoon of icing sugar into a bowl and whisk until the cream is thick but not buttery. Gently mix in the *fromage frais.* Refrigerate until needed.

On a flat surface cut 12 rounds from cooled sponge with an 8 cm (3¼ inch) round cutter. Slice each in half horizontally; cut each top round into 6 triangles.

Pipe three quarters of the cream filling on to the bottom rounds and cover with sliced strawberries. Pipe six rosettes of cream on top of each round. Halve reserved strawberries and slice each half into six slices. Support a triangle of sponge against each rosette and slip the strawberry slices between the triangles. Dust galettes with icing sugar.

# Lemon Curd Cakes

| | | |
|---|---|---|
| **Serves 12** | | **Calories**<br>170 |
| **Working<br>time: about<br>45 minutes** | | **Protein**<br>2g |
| | | **Cholesterol**<br>60mg |
| **Total time:<br>about<br>1 hour and<br>45 minutes** | | **Total fat**<br>4g |
| | | **Saturated fat**<br>2g |
| | | **Sodium**<br>25mg |

| | | |
|---|---|---|
| **3** | eggs | **3** |
| **1** | egg white | **1** |
| **125 g** | caster sugar | **4 oz** |
| **125 g** | plain flour | **4 oz** |
| **30 g** | unsalted butter, melted, cooled | **1 oz** |

| | | |
|---|---|---|
| **3 tbsp** | lemon curd | **3 tbsp** |
| | **Piped Frosting** | |
| **250 g** | caster sugar | **8 oz** |
| **1** | egg white | **1** |

Preheat oven to 180°C (350°F or Mark 4). Grease an oblong tin about 28 by 18 by 4 cm (11 by 7 by 1½ inches). Line base with parchment paper.

Put eggs, egg white and caster sugar in a bowl over a pan of hot, but not boiling, water on a low heat. Whisk eggs and sugar until thick and very pale. Remove bowl from heat and continue whisking until mixture is cool and leaves a trail. Sift flour lightly over top of whisked mixture and fold in carefully. Fold in the melted butter.

Pour sponge mixture into prepared tin and spread evenly. Bake sponge for 25 to 30 minutes, until well risen, firm to touch. Turn sponge out on a wire rack. Loosen but do not remove parchment paper. Place another rack on top of paper, invert both racks together so that paper is underneath. Remove top rack and leave to

cool. On a flat surface, slice in half horizontally and sandwich two layers with lemon curd.

Put sugar in a pan with 7.5 cl (2½ fl oz) of cold water. Heat gently until sugar has dissolved. Bring the syrup to the boil and cook it until its temperature reads 116°C (240°F) on a sugar thermometer. Whisk the egg white until it is very stiff but not dry. Immediately sugar syrup reaches required temperature, whisk into egg white, pouring in a steady stream from a height. Continue whisking until the frosting just loses its shine and becomes stiff enough to hold a peak.

Without delay, since the frosting will harden, within a few minutes, spoon the frosting into a piping bag with a seven-point 8 mm (⁵/₁₆th inch) star nozzle. Pipe frosting in a pattern on the cake, then cut into twelve when frosting is set.

# Chestnut and Chocolate Baskets

Makes 12
cakes

Working
time: about
1 hour and
10 minutes

Total time:
about
3 hours

Per cake:
Calories
230
Protein
4g
Cholesterol
60mg
Total fat
8g
Saturated fat
4g
Sodium
30mg

| | | |
|---|---|---|
| **325 g** | chestnut purée | **11 oz** |
| **3** | eggs, separated | **3** |
| **175 g** | caster sugar | **6 oz** |
| **250 g** | plain chocolate | **8 oz** |

| | | |
|---|---|---|
| **1** | egg white | **1** |
| **2 tbsp** | rum | **2 tbsp** |
| **180 g** | thick Greek yogurt | **6 oz** |
| **1 tsp** | icing sugar | **1 tsp** |

Preheat oven to 180°C (350°F or Mark 4). Grease twelve 10 cm (4 inch) tartlet tins and line base of each with parchment paper.

Whisk chestnut purée, egg yolks and 125 g (4 oz) of caster sugar in a bowl until mixture becomes very pale and thick. Melt 90 g (3 oz) of chocolate in a bowl over a pan of hot water. Let cool but not set; whisk into the chestnut mixture.

In another bowl, whisk whites until stiff but not dry. Whisk in remaining sugar to make meringue, gradually fold this into mixture.

Divide mixture equally among tins and level. Bake sponges for 15 to 20 minutes; a cocktail stick should come out clean when inserted in centre. Allow to cool in tins.

Chop 90 g (3 oz) of remaining chocolate. Put in bowl with rum over a pan of hot, not boiling water. Stir until chocolate melts and is blended with rum. Remove from heat. When cooled but not set, fold in yogurt.

Remove sponges from tins and peel off the paper. Place sponge rounds, spaced, on foil-lined baking sheets. Spread chocolate cream over tops of bases. Refrigerate until firm.

Cut out 12 strips of parchment paper, 2.5 cm (1 inch) wide and long enough to fit round chocolate bases with an overlap of about 1 cm (½ inch). Melt remaining chocolate and spread thinly over one strip of paper at a time, leaving 1 cm (½ inch) clear at one end for handling. Wrap the paper strip, chocolate side to cake, round each of the bases.

Sprinkle some chocolate shavings over the chocolate cream. Refrigerate cakes until chocolate is firmly set – about 1 hour – then peel away the paper. Dust icing sugar over the surfaces.

# Chocolate Sponges Coated in Coffee Cream

**Makes 10 sponges**

**Working time: about 1 hour and 15 minutes**

**Total time: about 2 hours and 15 minutes**

**Per sponge:**

Calories 210

Protein 4g

Cholesterol 80mg

Total fat 10g

Saturated fat 5g

Sodium 40mg

| | | |
|---|---|---|
| **3** | eggs | **3** |
| **1** | egg white | **1** |
| **125 g** | caster sugar | **4 oz** |
| **100 g** | plain flour | **3½ oz** |
| **15 g** | cocoa powder | **½ oz** |
| **90 g** | plain chocolate, coarsely grated | **3 oz** |

| | | |
|---|---|---|
| **20** | chocolate rose leaves | **20** |
| | **Coffee Cream** | |
| **60 g** | unsalted butter | **2 oz** |
| **1** | egg white | **1** |
| **90 g** | caster sugar | **3 oz** |
| **1 tbsp** | strong black coffee, cooled | **1 tbsp** |

Preheat oven to 180°C (350°F or Mark 4). Butter a 30 by 20 by 4 cm (12 by 8 by 1½ inch) oblong tin. Line the base with parchment paper.

Put eggs, egg white and caster sugar in a bowl over a pan of hot, but not boiling, water on a low heat. Whisk eggs and sugar until thick and very pale. Remove bowl from pan and whisk until mixture is cool and will hold a trail. Sift flour and cocoa very lightly over surface of whisked mixture and fold in gently, using a large metal spoon or a rubber spatula.

Pour sponge mixture into tin and level. Bake sponge for 25 to 30 minutes, until well risen, springy to touch and slightly shrunk from sides of tin. Turn sponge cake on to a wire rack. Loosen baking paper but do not remove it. Place another rack on top of paper, invert both racks

together so paper is underneath. Remove top rack and leave cake to cool.

Put butter into a bowl and beat well until light and fluffy. Put egg white and caster sugar in another bowl over a pan of water as before. Whisk the egg white and sugar together until they form a stiff, shiny meringue. Whisk meringue into butter to make a soft, fluffy cream, gradually beat in the coffee.

On a flat surface using an 8 cm (3¼ inch) plain oval cutter, cut out 10 ovals from sponge. Take one at a time and spread top with coffee cream. Decorate cream with a palette knife. Spread sides of each with a thin layer of coffee cream, press grated chocolate against sides. Decorate sponges with chocolate rose leaves, secured with a dab of coffee cream.

# Upside-Down Apple Ring

Serves 12

Working time: about 20 minutes

Total time: about 35 minutes

Calories 215
Protein 4g
Cholesterol 1mg
Total fat 10g
Saturated fat 2g
Sodium 175mg

| | | |
|---|---|---|
| 4 | digestive biscuits, crushed | 4 |
| 2 | dessert apples, peeled, cored and sliced | 2 |
| 125 g | polyunsaturated margarine | 4 oz |
| 90 g | dark brown sugar | 3 oz |
| 2 | egg whites, lightly beaten | 2 |

| | | |
|---|---|---|
| 15 cl | plain low-fat yogurt | ¼ pint |
| 250 g | wholemeal flour | 8 oz |
| 1 tsp | baking powder | 1 tsp |
| 1 tbsp | ground mixed spice | 1 tbsp |
| 1 | cooking apple, peeled, cored and grated | 1 |

Grease a 22 cm (9 inch) flat-based tube mould and sprinkle it with the biscuit crumbs to coat its inner surface. Arrange the apple slices in the base of the mould, overlapping them slightly.

In a large bowl, cream the margarine with the sugar, egg whites and yogurt. Sift in the flour with the baking powder and mixed spice, adding the bran left in the sieve. Fold the dry ingredients and the grated apple into the creamed mixture. Spoon the batter into the prepared ring mould and spread it evenly.

Microwave on medium high for 8 to 10 minutes, giving the dish a quarter turn every 2 minutes. The cake is cooked when it feels springy to the touch. Leave it to stand for 5 minutes before turning it out. Serve the apple ring warm or cold.

*Suggested accompaniment:* sweetened Greek yogurt.

# Grapefruit Cake

Serves 12

Working time: about 30 minutes

Total time: about 3 hours

Calories 240

Protein 4g

Cholesterol 65mg

Total fat 8g

Saturated fat 2g

Sodium 100mg

| | | | | | | |
|---|---|---|---|---|---|---|
| 125 g | sultanas | 4 oz | | 90 g | polyunsaturated margarine | 3 oz |
| 125 g | raisins | 4 oz | | 90 g | dark brown sugar | 3 oz |
| 125 g | currants | 4 oz | | 2 | large eggs, beaten | 2 |
| 1 | grapefruit, rind finely grated, flesh segmented and chopped | 1 | | 175 g | plain flour | 6 oz |
| 10 cl | fresh grapefruit juice | 3½ fl oz | | 1 tbsp | clear honey | 1 tbsp |

Grease the base of an 18 cm (7 inch) round cake dish and line it with greaseproof paper.

Put the sultanas, raisins, currants, grapefruit rind and juice in a bowl. Cover the fruit and microwave it on high for 3 minutes, stirring once. Remove the cover and leave the fruit to cool slightly.

Meanwhile, in another bowl, cream the margarine with the sugar and eggs until light and fluffy. Fold in the flour and the dried fruit mixture, blending well. Lastly, fold in the grapefruit flesh. Spoon the mixture into the cake dish and level the surface.

Cover the dish and place it on an inverted plate in the microwave. Cook the cake on high for 10 minutes, giving the dish a quarter turn every 3 minutes. Remove the cover, reduce the power to defrost and cook for a further 4 to 6 minutes – or until a skewer inserted into the centre of the cake comes out clean.

Leave the grapefruit cake to stand for 20 minutes before turning it out on to a wire rack to cool. While the cake is still warm, brush the top with the honey.

*Editor's Note:* One grapefruit will yield about 10 cl (3½ fl oz) of juice.